RAINFOREST
LIGHT AND SPIRIT

RAINFOREST
LIGHT AND SPIRIT

HARRY HOLCROFT
GHILLEAN PRANCE

Antique Collectors' Club

First published in Great Britain in 2009 by
ANTIQUE COLLECTORS' CLUB
Sandy Lane, Old Martlesham
Woodbridge, Suffolk
IP12 4SD

Text © Ghillean Prance, 2009
Diary entry text © Harry Holcroft, 2009
Illustrations © Harry Holcroft, 2009

www.harryholcroft.com

The moral right of the author and illustrator
has been asserted

A CIP catalogue record for this book is available from the British Library.

ISBN 978-1-85149-577-1

Printed in Spain

Tributary, Upper Amazon, Colombia.

CONTENTS

www.harryholcroft.com

RAINFOREST FLORA AND FAUNA
by GHILLEAN PRANCE

8

Saal forest, India.

The world's rainforests are not just the richest source of biodiversity on Earth, they are also entire eco-systems of incomparable mystery and beauty, as well as providing the "air-conditioning system" and rainfall patterns for the entire world. More than forty tribes are thought to exist in the Amazon basin alone which have yet to make contact with the outside world, and although about a quarter of all modern medicines come from rainforest plants, it is thought we have only discovered a fraction of the species available.

This book, with its combination of evocative painting and prose, is a tribute to that mystery and beauty and I can only congratulate Harry Holcroft and Sir Ghillean Prance for capturing both in such a remarkable way.

I started my own Rainforests Project in October 2007 because I fear for the future of the critical life support system they represent in the face of rapidly accelerating deforestation brought about by the demand for beef, soya, palm oil and timber. The simple truth is that we depend on the rainforests for our very existence – to a far greater extent than perhaps many of us realize. Not only do they store carbon more efficiently and effectively than anything else on this Earth, but they also generate the rainfall that grows the crops which feed the world. But every year when they are burnt, they release more carbon dioxide into the atmosphere than all of the world's cars, aeroplanes and ships put together. So their preservation is utterly critical for our climate stability, food and medicine; their destruction threatens our very life on Earth. That is why we must - each of us - strain every sinew to ensure the survival of the remaining rainforests. This excellent book is, in itself, a powerful advocate and call to arms. For the sake of our children and grandchildren, and for the sake of that very biodiversity on which, often unconsciously, we all depend, I pray that we may all heed its message…

INTRODUCTION

Artist Harry Holcroft has visited many of the tropical equatorial rainforests of the world in his quest to paint images of this wonderful ecosystem. With the typical observational powers of an artist he has noticed considerable differences in the physiognomy and biology in the forests of the different continents he has visited. This text is an attempt to explain some of the reasons why, although there are striking similarities between different areas, the rainforest is not a single uniform type of vegetation. The differences between regions are both historic and biological. Even within regions there is much variation to be seen by the visitor who travels around the Amazon region, the Congo Basin or the island of Borneo. This is mainly due to local variations in climate, soil, flooding regime and topography.

Here I shall discuss some of the regional variations and the similarities and differences between the great rainforests of America, Africa and Malaysia based on the history, the vegetation, and some of the striking plants and animals that are to be found in these forests. We also aim to stress the vital importance of the world's rainforests both as a source of biodiversity and due to their role in stabilising climate. No account of the rainforests of the world would be complete without something about the wonderful indigenous people who have learned to live in, and sustainably manage, them.

The artist sees the differences in the colour produced both by the light and by the diversity of the greens and blues of the vegetation. The scientist brings out some of the spirit of the rainforest through its diversity and its plant, animal and human inhabitants.

Professor Sir Ghillean Prance

Macaws, the Pantanel, Brazil.

Part I

CHARACTERISTICS AND DISTRIBUTION OF RAINFORESTS

Tropical rainforests occur in a rather narrow belt near to the equator in areas where there is a large rainfall (usually at least 2000 mm) and a climate that is not too seasonal. True rainforest is tall and evergreen and the canopy and emergent trees have rather straight trunks that do not branch until 30m or more because it makes little sense to produce leaves under the canopy where there is so little light. Many of the trees have buttressed trunks, an adaptation to make them more stable, while their shallow spreading root systems reabsorb the available nutrients in an impressive recycling system. Another feature of rainforest trees is the sharply pointed 'drip tip' on the leaves, an adaptation that allows the heavy rainfall to run off easily without damaging the leaves.

The height of the dense forest canopy varies from site to site. Above are the emergent trees that tower above the green carpet of the canopy, while underneath there grows a host of smaller trees, shrubs and herbs adapted to the low light intensity. Many of the trees are often woven together by an abundance of woody vines or lianas.

The tree species in a rainforest have two different strategies for growth: they are either shade tolerant or light demanding. The shade tolerant species grow steadily and often slowly under the shade until they reach the canopy. The light demanding species need more light and have to wait until a tree falls and creates a light gap in the forest. They then shoot up rapidly, trying to occupy as much of the space as possible. Many of the colonising species are light demanding, but also many of the primary forest trees, such as the Brazil nut (*Bertholletia excelsa*) of the Amazon forest, exhibit this strategy.

The forest changes visibly according to the altitude – at the highest levels is cloud forest with the tree branches covered with dripping wet mosses. This transition can readily be seen along the fringes of the Andes or on Mount Cameroon in Africa and Mount Kinabalu in Borneo. As one moves away from the equator the weather generally becomes drier and more seasonal, and so the rainforest is replaced by seasonal semi-deciduous forest, open savanna woodland or grassland savanna, depending on other local features.

The Main Areas of Tropical Rainforest

IN SOUTH AMERICA the Amazon Basin holds the largest single area of rainforest. This extends into parts of Bolivia, Brazil, Colombia, Ecuador, Peru, Venezuela and the three Guianas. Rainforest patches can also be found north through Central America into southern Mexico, and there is also an important belt of rainforest to the west of the Andes in the Chocó of Colombia that extends south into northern Ecuador. There is also a very rich area of rainforest that stretches in a narrow belt along the Atlantic coast of Brazil. Over 50 percent of the tree species and many animals are endemic to the *mata atlantica*, but unfortunately only six percent of the original area of this rainforest remains intact and so it is not surprising that it is one of the designated hotspots for conservation priority.

Banyan tree, Kerala, Southern India.

Macaws amongst drip-tip foliage.

In Africa the largest block of rainforest is that of the Congo Basin. There is also a considerable area of rainforest or former rainforest in West Africa, which, apart from a natural gap in Togo and Benin, extends west as far as the Atlantic coast. The Congo forests remain relatively intact, but those of West Africa are largely destroyed.

In the Far East rainforests occur in India, Sri Lanka, Burma, Thailand, Australia and in the biogeographic region called Malesia, consisting of Peninsular Malaysia, the Philippines, Borneo, Indonesia, New Guinea and the Solomon Islands. In this whole region rainforest forms a relatively consistent unit, although there is much local variation. The rainforest of Asia extends quite far northwards into southwestern China, and at 26°N it is one of the most distant rainforests from the equator. This is made possible by moisture bearing warm winds from the ocean.

Biological Diversity

Although rainforest occupies about six percent of the total land area of the world, it houses well over 50 percent of all species of organisms. Recent studies in both Western Amazonia and in the Atlantic coastal forests of Brazil have shown that a single hectare of forest (2.5 acres) can contain up to 300 species of trees with trunk diameters of 10 centimetres or more. And that is only the trees! There are also many herbs and shrubs, as well as the epiphytes, that use the trees as perches.

A study of a 0.1 hectare plot of forest in Peru found a total of 283 species of trees and lianas. Another study in Costa Rica of all the plants in a 100m² plot (less than half a tennis court) found 233 species of vascular plants in it.

Some areas of rainforest are richer than others in their species content and this has been shown to be largely connected to the amount and the seasonality of rainfall. Drier areas are generally not as diverse as wetter areas, which is why western Amazonia near to the Andes, where there is a huge rainfall and no real dry season, is so species diverse. It has been shown that the diversity of plant species in a given area increases with increasing rainfall up to about 9,000mm of annual rainfall, but that above this amount of rainfall there is little or no increase in plant diversity.

Biological Connections between Rainforest Areas

Today, the three main blocks of rainforest are widely separated geographically, so it not surprising that there are differences which can be spotted by a painter. However, biologists are often more interested in the similarities that indicate a common origin for the plants and animals that inhabit rainforests. For plants, many of the same families and even genera are to be found in each region. As a specialist in the Amazon flora I had little difficulty in identifying the families and many of the genera when I travelled in Africa or Asia. On the other hand, few of the species are familiar. Only a very few species occur in both Africa and South America. One, *Parinari excelsa,* the African greenheart in the family Chrysobalanaceae, is widespread in the rainforests of both Africa and South America.

There are two main reasons for the floristic similarities between the forests of different continents: the ability of some plants to disperse over long distances, and a shared history at some time in the past. It is easy, for example, to see why the cocoa plum (*Chrysobalanus icaco*) occurs around the coastal shores of West Africa and the coasts of the Caribbean and eastern South America, and extends inland a short way into the forests of both continents. This is a shoreline species, the seeds of which remain viable for a short while in salt water and whose juicy fruits are eaten by birds. It is not surprising that this species has found its way from one continent to another by long-distance dispersal. Over the many million years of separation of the major rainforests some species have been able to travel across the oceans, carried by birds, wind or by ocean currents. This probably explains how a single species of the cactus genus *Rhipsalis* reached Africa. The cacti are characteristically New World plants and, except for the one species of *Rhipsalis baccifera*, they have only been introduced elsewhere by humans. The species *R. baccifera* occurs in Africa, Madagascar and Sri Lanka. A similar event has also happened in the Bromeliaceae (pineapple) family, which has over two thousand species in the Americas and a single species, *Pitcairnia feliciana*, in a sandstone area of West Africa. This species has been shown to be very similar to the South American species of *Pitcairnia* and so it is obvious that long distance dispersal took place at some time in the not too remote past.

A tree species that occurs in both Africa and South America is the anani (*Symphonia globulifera*) in the Clusiaceae (Saint-John's-wort) family. This tree has a distinctive yellow sap and scarlet flowers that are often found in great masses under the trees. The kapok tree, *Ceiba pentandra,* occurs in both the American and African rainforests. A recent molecular study showed very few genetic differences between the American and African populations, which would indicate a relatively recent dispersal from one continent to the other. Since all the close relatives of the kapok occur in South America it seems certain that this species travelled in an easterly direction from South America to Africa. Kapok has wind dispersed seeds that are embedded in a buoyant fibre and so it is likely that some seeds of this species were carried across the ocean in a storm at some time in the not too distant past.

Long-distance dispersal has been important, but many of the biological similarities between the different blocks of rainforest must be due to a common history. We now know that continents have moved around through the tectonic process of continental drift, and that in the past the rainforest regions of the world were much closer together.

AFRICA AND SOUTH AMERICA – at the time when the flowering plants or angiosperms began to diversify, about 140 million years ago, Africa and South America were joined together on the ancient land mass of Gondwanaland and it was a long time before the continents were separated by a great distance. This meant that many of the early ancestors of present day rainforest plants were distributed on what were then two scarcely separated continents, and they were able to cross the short distances between the gradually separating land masses. Initially, there were certainly islands between the drifting continents which also aided the dispersal of organisms. As a result most of the plant families are to be found in both Africa and America; for example, Caesalpiniaceae, Moraceae and Sapotaceae abound on both continents.

In some cases, the separation has been long enough for the representatives of a plant family on one continent to be subdivided in a separate subfamily from those of the other continent. The Brazil nut family, Lecythidaceae, occurs in all three rainforest continents and all except one species of the South American ones belong to the

Saal rainforest, Madhya Pradesh, Northern India. This is where Rudyard Kipling first heard the Hindu word 'jungle', which he introduced to the West.

subfamily Lecythidoideae whereas the African ones are mostly placed in a subfamily named the Napoleonaeoideae and those of Malaysia in the subfamily Planchonioideae. The ancestors of the Lecythidaceae have been separated long enough for differentiation to have taken place at the subfamilial level.

AFRICA AND ASIA — There is good fossil evidence that African and Asian rainforests were more or less connected in the early Tertiary Period, about 55 million years ago until about 30 million years ago. These two regions were linked by a continuous forest belt because of a warmer and moister climate than that of the present. Since this connection was much more recent than the connection between Africa and South America, the flora of the African forests shares more similarity with those of Asia than of South America. This relationship is also apparent in various animals. The African and the Asian primates belong to a group called the Catarrhines, whereas the monkeys of South America are so different that they are classified in a different group called the Platyrhines many of which have prehensile tails.

AUSTRALIA, NEW GUINEA AND ASIA — Australia and New Guinea were also originally a part of Gondwanaland, but this fragment separated from that land mass at about the same time as South America. In addition, it did not have a climate suitable for rainforest until a much later date. Once it did, the forests became composed of the groups of plants that were able to reach this new area by dispersal. This region evolved its own quite distinct rainforest flora and fauna. For example, various ancient cone-bearing plants adapted to the rainforest as exemplified by the genus *Agathis*. As the Australasian plate drifted northwards and became more tropical it collided with the Asian plate in the Tertiary Period, about 35 million years ago. The area consisting of Malaysia, Sumatra, Borneo and Java is known as Sundaland. This rafting of the land united two different floras and faunas and some crossover occurred as plants and animals migrated between the areas of Asian and Australasian origin. The biological difference is still distinct enough that British naturalist Alfred Russel Wallace (1823-1913) defined a distinct boundary between Sundaland and Australasia that has come to be named the Wallace Line. The intermediate area between Sundaland and Australasia, where considerable exchange of flora and fauna has taken place, is termed Wallacea and includes the Philippines, Sulawesi, the Moluccas and Timor. Because of his extensive travels in Amazonia and Malaysia, Wallace came to the theory of evolution by natural selection and the survival of the fittest quite independently of Charles Darwin.

The genus *Agathis* is unusual because it is the most tropical of all conifers with many species being true denizens of the rainforest. It is distributed from Sumatra and Malaya through Indonesia to Queensland (Australia) and across the Pacific to Fiji and New Caledonia, also with a single species (*A. australis*) in the North Island of New Zealand. The species of *Agathis* are characteristic of forests without a marked dry season. Two species of *Agathis* occur in the white sand of heath forest, *A. borneensis* in Borneo and *A. labillardierei* in New Guinea. *Agathis* furnishes a high-grade timber and is also much exploited for copal resin. Some trees of *Agathis microstachya* in the forests of Queensland are estimated to be one thousand years old.

THE PITCHER PLANT – A characteristic genus of plants in Malaysia is the carnivorous pitcher plant *Nepenthes,* which has about 80 different species there. It is interesting that a single species of *Nepenthes* occurs in Madagascar and another, *N. pervillei,* in the Seychelles. This is a good example of long-distance dispersal from one major region to another. Madagascar has received a good number of plant species through dispersal from the Asian region.

The large jug-like pitchers of *Nepenthes* are actually modified leaves and they contain an enzyme-rich liquid. When an insect or a small animal has the misfortune to tumble into this trap it is gradually digested, providing essential nutrients to the plant. Carnivory in plants is

Nepenthes *(pitcher plant), Borneo.*

generally an adaptation to low-nutrient habitats. Most, such as the familiar sundews and butterworts of Europe, occur in bogs but many of the species of *Nepenthes* are to be found in the forests and mountains of tropical Asia and Malesia. (Malesia is a term used by biogeographers for the tropical Asian region including Peninsular Malaysia, Borneo, Indonesia, the Philippines, New Guinea and the Solomon Islands.) There they occur in the sandy heath forests, wet peat swamps and in open areas along roadsides where nutrients are scarce. They also are common on the higher mountains. Species of *Nepenthes* can grow from sea level up to an altitude of about 3,000m in Borneo, where *Nepethes rajah* and *N. villo*sa occur on Mount Kinabalu. Of the 80 species, the majority of *Nepenthes* are terrestrial or climbers, but a few, such as *N. veitchii* are often epiphytic. The largest pitcher, which can hold up to two litres of water, is that of the magnificent *Nepethes rajah* (named after Rajah Brooke of Sarawak). *Nepenthes merrilliana* from the Philippines is a near competitor for it also has an extremely large pitcher. There are no pitcher plants in the forests of Africa and America, but the South American pitcher plant, *Sarracenia,* grows in the bogs of the high table mountains of Venezuela and the Guianas.

The rainforest of Madagascar today only occurs in the moister northeastern part of the island, while much of the rest of the country is covered by more arid types of vegetation. This large island separatedfrom Africa about 140 million years ago in the Jurassic Period. While the flora and fauna show closest relations with Africa, they are very different because isolation has allowed evolution to proceed independently for such a long time.

Eighty five percent of the plant species of Madagascar are endemic to that island. However, at the family level, they still fit into the plant families of the other rainforest areas. Only the family Humbertiaceae is endemic to Madagascar and, again, I was able to identify easily most of the families of plants there. There are so many endemic genera of plants in Madagascar, that these are harder for the Amazonian expert to distinguish. At the time the island separated, there were some primate ancestors present which have evolved into a very distinct

Kingfisher, Iguaçu Falls, Paraguay.

group – the lemurs. Lemurs were distributed widely throughout warmer regions of the world during the Eocene epoch, but today they survive only in Madagascar. This is probably because the isolation of Madagascar from Africa in the Tertiary Period left it with no native carnivores and, therefore, the lemurs with no predators.

In summary, we can say that the present day organisms of rainforests had a common origin on the supercontinent of Gondwanaland about 140 million years ago, during the Jurassic Period. At that time there were only the more primitive ancestors of the modern flora and fauna around and the angiosperm or seed plants had only just begun to develop. Since the separation of the areas occurred at different times, the various relationships of today's fauna and flora vary from area to area largely depending upon the length of isolation between any two areas, but also according to the capacity of some organisms for long-distance dispersal. A common evolutionary heritage has developed over time into the amazing diversity that is the tropical rainforest as we know it today.

Tuesday, 6th February, 2007
The Miri River, Borneo

Fast Food in the Jungle

One of the Iban Tribe's periodic pastimes used to be taking a hunting party to collect neighbour's heads.!

Population pressure in the jungle was such that headhunting was the natural form of population control.

Hunting parties would consist of 5 or 6 able-bodied 'Warrior Lads' on a 3-4 day romp through the woods. No luggage could be taken, as a suitable number of heads had to be brought back. Water could be found en route and so all that was required were weapons and handfuls of dry rice that they carried in bags slung round their necks for food.

In the woods they would select suitable 'pitcher plants' to use as a sort of Jungle 'takeaway'. The pitcher plants in question are big. They attract large bugs, and frogs which, drawn by the mucus and scent, jump onto the 'lid' of the plant. The plant then 'flicks' the frog/bug into its bowel or cavity and, shutting its lid, begins to digest them.

The warriors would appear, take a handful of dried rice from the pouches around their necks and drop them into the plants.

The plant, tricked into thinking that it has caught a large meal, and not knowing that this is someone else's food, starts digesting the rice.

Three days later, our warriors return through the forest with their haul of trophy heads. In the meantime, the pitcher plant has been working overtime to digest the rice, in effect 'slow cooking' it together with other frog/bug type proteins - a perfect 'Fast Food Takeaway' - free of charge - is ready on arrival.

The modified leaf of the Nepenthes *forms a jug-like shape, into which small animals and insects are attracted, then trapped and digested by the plant.*

Variations within the Amazon Rainforest

The Amazon rainforest together with that of the Orinoco Basin is by far the largest area of continuous rainforest in the world. There are many local variations due to variation in rainfall and soil conditions.

The size and the variation of the Amazon region enable a number of quite distinct forest types to exist. The tall rainforest on non-flooded, well-drained soils is generally known as terra firme forest and this is by far the most abundant forest type in the region. It generally has a canopy at about 30m, but some emergent trees such as the Brazil nut (*Bertholletia excelsa*) and the angelim pedra (*Dinizia excelsa*) can reach up to 55m in height.

There are large areas of Amazonia and smaller ones in the Congo forests that are subject to periodical inundation as river level rises in the rainy season. In central Amazonia the difference in water level between the high and low water season of the rivers can be as much as 15m. This means that there are extensive areas of floodplain forests. These have many different plant species from the terra firme forests and they are not as species diverse. In Brazil, areas flooded by the sediment-rich white-water rivers are termed *várzea* forest and those inundated by the acidic black water are called *igapó*. There are considerable differences in species composition and physiognomy between these two types of seasonally inundated forest.

A characteristic tree of the várzea forest is the silk cotton or kapok tree (*Ceiba pentandra*) in the Bombacaceae family. This is a giant of these white water flooded forests of Amazonia. It is the tallest tree beside many rivers and has a characteristic umbrella-like crown. The flowers are pollinated by bats and when its large ovoid fruits develop, they are filled by a fibre that surrounds the seeds. The fruits split open to release showers of white fluff or kapok, which floats in the air and disperses the seeds that are embedded in this cottony mass of fibres, thereby accounting for how this species also reached Africa. The young trunk of the kapok tree is spinous but these thorns have completely disappeared by the time the tree matures. This adaptation must have evolved as a protection from predators for the young tree

The acidic black waters — igapó — of the River Negro, a tributary of the Amazon, Brazil.

that is no longer necessary as the tree becomes well established. The large crotches of the branches of the *Ceiba* tree are the favourite nesting site of the majestic harpy eagle (*Harpia harpyia*), the largest bird of the Amazon forest. Another member of the Bombacaceae, *Pachira aquatica*, is also a common species in seasonally flooded areas. Some other typical species of the *várzea* forest include the ucuuba (*Virola surinamensis*), a much sought after timber tree, and the rubber tree (*Hevea brasiliensis*), as well as several species of figs (*Ficus*).

Where there is more permanent water swamp forest may occur. This is relatively rare in Amazonia, but abundant in Borneo where there is a lot of peat swamp with the forest growing over the top. In 1983 there was a period of drought in Borneo and there were serious fires as the peat dried out and caught light as a result of slash and burn agriculture. This killed many trees as well as releasing a huge amount of carbon dioxide into the atmosphere. Clearing of peat forest continues even today and in 2007 peat fires were occurring in Sumatra.

Scattered throughout Amazonia, but more abundantly in the Basin of the Rio Negro, are areas of bleached white sands. This soil type is very poor in nutrients and so the vegetation is low and scrubby with many gnarled and twisted trees full of epiphytes. This type of vegetation is known as *caatinga* or *campina* in Brazil. Very similar to *caatinga* are the heath forests, or *kerangas* of Borneo. This type of vegetation also occurs on white sand and looks almost identical to *campina*. Both of these white sand vegetation types are characterized by the thick leathery leaves of the trees and shrubs that are full of tannins and other phenolic compounds. This is a defense mechanism to reduce insect predation and hence the loss of nutrients in this nutrient poor ecosystem.

There are some areas of Amazonia where the forest is more open and the trees are covered with a large number of vines or lianas. This liana forest or *cipoal* is abundant in southern Amazonia and in Roraima State. In western Amazonia in the State of Acre and in neighboring Peru there are large areas of bamboo forest where giant bamboos clamber over the trees. It is probable that both liana forests and bamboo forests are due to disturbances in the past either by climate changes or human activity.

Giant bamboo, Upper Amazon, Peru.

Kapok trees,
Upper Amazon,
Peru.

Rainforest and the Artist

Why has no-one effectively painted rainforest or the tropics in either Western culture or the East?

Perhaps there are two reasons: artists who dedicate their lives to painting have generally remained poor. Consequently, they have been unable to travel to different lands. But poverty is not an insuperable barrier to a good determined artist.

The more powerful reason is that the rainforest is simply too difficult - if not 'unpaintable'.

Part of the Iguaçu Falls, Paraguay, South America.

34

Excess, chaos and daunting complexity confront the artist. He is bullied, robbed of initiative, dictated to. There seems to be no room in the painting for the profusion that exists. A painter has to begin by leaving nine tenths of reality out of the picture. This is what Gaugin and Rousseau did. If not, there would be no 'seeing the wood from the inordinate quantity of trees'.

No artist so far seems to have told us how Rainforest should be seen. These 'corridors of green and leech-infested shadow' we know only from a photograph or the holiday eco-brochure. Yet there is something more subtle, something we all dimly know, yet have not grasped.

Peepol trees, Madhya Pradesh, Northern India.

The English landscape was beautiful before Constable or Gainsborough painted it, but they made the loveliness clearly visible, giving it name and definition.

Until now our best definition of 'Rainforest' has been in literature. Conrad gives us the reality of the rainforest, in Heart of Darkness; as do Kipling and Melville in their works. But for the painter, how is it to be done?

Rainforest disorientates. You are lost. But not in the physical sense. The absolute self-sufficiency of the forest confuses the sense of purpose and self-esteem. This is a living entity.

For the painter there is no perspective, no vanishing point, no control of form, no logic to the play of light, no logic to the play of tone, and no logic to the play of space, no composition... In short: chaos!

Yet, like Gainsborough, we need to give it name and definition. We must find order in the chaos. Capture the essence and make it understandable to the viewer.

And so, how?

And so, Jackson Pollock

Look: and perceive chaos or order in Pollock's Lavender Mist

Jackson Pollock, Lavender Mist: Number 1, *1950*
(National Gallery of Art, Washington DC, USA/The Bridgeman Art Library; ©ARS, NY and DACS, London 2008.

Chaos – Order – Reason

The human mind craves for order. The whole pursuit of art, music, and literature is to find vital form or spiritual meaning within the desperate array of the material world.

Yet try and paint rainforest - complete chaos.

My favourite artists are the early Flemish. They strived to find order in the Renaissance world.

When painting rainforest, Jackson Pollock has been my inspiration.

Look at his Abstract Expressionism and at first you see chaos, but then look deeper, and you see wonderful order, control and discipline.

Toucan, Peru, South America.

Saturday, 24th March, 2007
The Pantanal, Brazil

The changing wisdom of successive generations discards
ideas, questions facts, demolishes theories. But the artist
appeals to that part of our being which is not dependent
on wisdom; to that in us which is a gift not an acquisition.
He speaks to our capacity for delight and wonder, to the
mystery surrounding our lives, to our sense of pity, beauty,
pain; to the latent feeling of fellowship with all creation,
to the subtle convictions of solidarity that binds the
human condition, in dreams, in joy, in sorrow, in
aspirations, in illusion, in hope and fear, to that which
binds all human kind - the dead to the living and the
living to the unborn.

And so the artist taps in to the secret spring of responsive
emotions to touch our common consciousness.

But how does the painter achieve this?

Good paintings come about, more often than not, by
accident and acute vigilance for what is worth preserving,
rather than by consultation in a design process.

The wetlands of the Pantanal, Brazil, South America.

Rainforest and Religion

Monotheism came from the barren - the living faiths of the West come from the desert. Walk amongst the mountains of the Sinai and you understand why God talked to Moses. They are not big like the Alps or the Andes, but they stand stark and menacing from the desert. From Moses and Abraham comes Judaism, Christianity and, finally, Islam. Even Zoroastrianism, the first of monotheistic ideas, came from the barren plains and rocks of Persia.

But what of the tropics and the rainforest? Monotheism is the last belief that could come to the mind of man living near the Equator. In a tropical jungle only a blind, deaf mute could be monotheist.

The woods are horrible. They teem with countless small and individual mysteries. Unaccountable sights in the half darkness. Inexplicable sounds across the silence. In a jungle, nobody with eyes, ears, smell, touch and taste can fail to believe in spirits, ghosts and devils...

Peepol trees, Madhya Pradesh, Northern India.

H.St.J.Holcroft

The Human Spirit

With all our talk of the destruction of the environment, after a lifetime of travelling the world, I personally feel a far greater concern for the destruction of the human spirit.

Man has evolved in the natural environment. Ethnology (the study of primitive peoples), plus present day observation of rural societies, all point to men naturally congregating into 'village' communities. The essential nature of these communities is that the actions of each individual are known to all others. Consequently, honesty and charity become the best policy - values encompassed by all major faiths.

If all statistics are to be believed, over half the human race now lives in cities. There are already twenty cities with populations of over ten million. In this new unnatural urban environment, the individual is anonymous and solitary in the crowd and so honesty and charity cease to be of such importance.

The disturbing effect of urbanisation appears to be this: a migrant world population of men and women, who live in no place long enough to become attached to it, or influenced by its spirit. They have no real connection to land - unlike the village communities in the rainforest - but rely on the convenient symbol of money; they have few children and appear to believe in no organised religion. They are compelled by this urban life to impose enormous strain on their own resources of mind and will, in personal relationships with their fellow human beings - in love, marriage, friendship and family ties. They have nothing solid on which they can lean. The strain is often more than their spiritual resources and their personal relationships can bear.

Hence dissatisfaction, a shallowness of life and a profound uncertainty of purpose.

Highland forest, Malaysia.

Orchid, Mauritius, Indian Ocean.

Part II

DIFFERENCES BETWEEN THE RAINFOREST AREAS

The Danum Valley, Borneo,
one of the only remaining areas
of true primary rainforest.

We have seen above that the history of the three major blocks of rainforest have been rather different over time. All three areas are similar enough for even an amateur to know that they are in a rainforest as opposed to another type of vegetation. They all have an amazing diversity of species and a general cathedral-like appearance with tall evergreen trees, lianas and epiphytes that would classify them as rainforest. However, closer analysis also reveals many differences as well.

The Varying Effects of Climate Change

In the more recent prehistoric times the climate has changed naturally several times. We now know that there have been periods of cooler and drier weather in Amazonia associated with periods of glaciation in the northern and southern temperate regions. The result of this is that the amount of contiguous rainforest has fluctuated from age to age. The last cooler period was about 18,000 years ago in the time known as the Last Glacial Maximum (LGM). Some areas that are now covered by rainforest were replaced by semi-deciduous forest and savanna. We know about this history from studies of fossilised pollen grains found in the deposits of various lakes in the region. The ratio of different types of pollen from known dates enables the reconstruction of the past history. The exact distribution of forest versus other types of vegetation is uncertain because the data are incomplete. However, it has been estimated that the humid rainforest in Amazonia was reduced to about 54 percent of its present-day extension at the time of the LGM. In contrast, it is thought that the rainforest of the Congo Basin in Africa was probably reduced by as much as 84 percent. This historic difference between these areas is one of the reasons for different characteristics of these two major blocks of forest.

Fishing boat with sails made of palm leaves,
Miri River in Dipterocarp forest, Borneo.

Even today much of the Amazonian forest has a moister climate than that of Africa. In Africa there is an additional factor, that the degree of human disturbance of the forest has been much greater than in South America. However, in both continents areas that appear to be virgin rainforest often show signs of human disturbance when detailed studies are made.

The effect of climate changes has not been so great in the Asian rainforests, but one of the main differences is that these forests are on a series of islands in the archipelago of Indonesia, New Guinea and associated islands. The times of glaciation affected this region in a different way because a great amount of water was tied up in the glacial ice and sea levels were much lower than today. This meant that many of today's islands in Malesia were linked to each other by land and vegetation. This explains the general biological similarity across such a broad region. One might have expected there to have been evolution of more differences between the fauna and flora on the different islands, but these past land links have allowed dispersal to continue until relatively recent times. Studies of pollen and other evidence shows that the more usual state of Malesia over the past two million years has been as a single land mass rather that an archipelago. The channel separating Sundaland from New Guinea where Wallace's Line occurs is a deeper channel and this has slowed the merging of the floras of Asia and Australasia because there was never a dry land connection.

DIFFERENT FLORA ACROSS THE REGIONS

Dipterocarps

The forests of Malesia tend to be taller than those of Amazonia with the canopy often at 35–40m and the emergent trees reaching to 60–70m in height. The most striking difference of the Asian rainforests over those of other areas is that the forests are dominated by a single family of trees, the Dipterocarpaceae. This family abounds in India,

Sri Lanka, throughout Malesia, and a few species have even dispersed into New Guinea across Wallace's Line. The dipterocarps are striking for the abundance of species in Malesia and for their size and number of individuals in the forest. Many emergents are dipterocarps that rise above the canopy and give the characteristic appearance of Malesian rainforests. Harry Holcroft has commented to me that the forests of Malesia have a more primeval appearance than those of Africa and Amazonia. This is largely due to a combination of the more stable history of the Asiatic region and the dominance and height of the dipterocarps.

There is no good explanation why this family has been so successful and has evolved into so many species. Pollen data show that there was a sudden increase in dipterocarp pollen about 30 million years ago. The Malesian and Indian members of this family belong to the subfamily Dipterocarpoideae. A few species of dipterocarps occur in Africa where they are trees of savanna and woodland rather than rainforest and they belong to the subfamily Monotoideae. A single genus of dipterocarps, with only two species (*Pakaraima*), occurs in the highlands of Venezuela. How *Pakaraima* got there remains a mystery and it is classified in a separate subfamily of the Dipterocarpaceae, the Pakaraimoideae. With this distribution it seems that the dipterocarps must have originated in Gondwana. Their abundance in Sri Lanka and the fact that they diversified explosively about 30 million years ago indicates that they were carried to Asia on the drifting plate of India and Sri Lanka. After that collided with Asia they spread and speciated rapidly. In Malesia the downfall of the dipterocarps is that they yield an excellent timber and so have been over exploited in many areas such as the Philippines and Borneo so that some species are now threatened with extinction.

Another unusual feature of the dipterocarps is their mast fruiting. Similar to the beech trees of England the dipterocarps flower and fruit only in occasional years. It is thought that this is associated with periodic droughts. Mast fruiting floods the forest with seeds in some years and produces little in others. This confuses seed predators because of the inconsistent availability of food and it also keeps the predator population at lower levels. When there is a mast fruiting so many seeds are produced that many escape predation.

SHOREA is the largest genus of dipterocarps with about 194 species distributed from Sri Lanka and southern India through the Malay Peninsula to the Philippines and Molucca Islands. It is the dominant emergent tree genus of the lowland forests of Sundaland as well as the most important timber genus. The commercial name for many species of *Shorea* is meranti in Malaya. Species of *Shorea* occur in other types of forest such as riverine forest and peat swamps and a few even occur in montane forest up to 1,750m (e.g. *Shorea brunnescens*, in the mountains of Borneo). Species of dipteropcarps are often used to define the different forest types of Malesia. For example, hill dipterocarp forest of Malaysia, which occurs between elevations of 300 and 800 metres, is characterised by the presence of *Shorea curtisii*. Typical of upper dipterocarp forest from 800–1200m is *Shorea platyclados*, an important source of timber. *Shorea albida* is a characteristic species of heath forests and white sand soil. *Shorea macrophylla* and some other species produce little nuts called illipes which contain a fat used as a substitute for cocoa butter and is also used locally in soap, candles, and as a medicine. In Borneo the nuts are collected by local people for subsistence use as a flavouring, cooking oil and medical salve. Illipe is also a commercial product of considerable value and in 1989 almost 14,000 tonnes (worth US $5million) were exported from West Kalimantan in Indonesia.

Kingfishers, Madagascar.

The Colours of the Rainforest

As I travelled the rainforests of the world there was something naggingly different about the Amazon - Africa - India - Borneo.

As an artist, I was desperately looking to find this difference. I felt passionately that there was a difference. I was thinking: form; shape; spacial...
And like so many things in our lives it was staring me in the face, so simple, so obvious and yet to human foolishness, obscure. Until, in Borneo, it hit me like a sledgehammer:

It was colour...

Borneo is blue because of the amount of water vapour in the atmosphere...

India is yellow because of the dust and smoke from a vast population burning fuel ...

The Amazon is green because geologically it is new and still very healthy... The Amazonian Indians have 15 different words for the colour green!

Malaysian Palm.

Palm forest, Bolivia.

IN MALESIA the majestic giant fish tail palm (*Caryota maxima*) can reach 35m in height in the mid montane forests of Malesia, and has a characteristic appearance because of its doubly pinnate leaves. It is one of the monocarpic palms, meaning that it grows steadily until it flowers, and then after flowering once and producing many seeds, it dies. The stems are used to extract sago. There are about 12 species of *Caryota* occurring from Sri Lanka, India, southern China through Malesia to Queensland, and the Solomon Islands.

IN ASIA the forests are characterised by the abundant presence of rattan palms. These are unusual for palms because they are vines that sprawl over the trees. Rattans have very spiny trunks, but inside is the cane that is so useful for basket work and furniture. As a result, they have been much over exploited from the forest and some species are becoming rare. There over 600 species of rattans in Malesia. Rattans also occur in the forests of Africa but are much less common and have only 22 species. In the South American rainforests there are no rattans, but another rarer genus of vining palms *Desmoncus* occurs and is also sometimes used for its cane in Venezuela. This genus has reflexed, fish hook-like spines on the end of the leaves that enable it to catch onto other vegetation as it climbs up.

IN MADAGASCAR *Ravenea musicalis,* newly discovered by Henk Bentje, is interesting because it is truly aquatic. The seeds germinate under the water of the river and, before a trunk forms, the seedling leaves float in the water. No other palm has ever been found with this habit.

There are two species of palms with an aquatic habit adapted to mangrove forests. In Asia, the Nypa palm (*Nypa fruiticans*) is found from the Bay of Bengal through to Australia and the Solomon Islands. The fossil record shows that this species was once much more widely distributed in Europe, Africa and India. *Nypa* is an acaulescent palm, meaning that it does not have a trunk so the rosette of leaves emerges directly from the soil or water. In South America, a palm with a similar adaptation to this salt water habitat is *Raphia taedigera.*

Several genera of palms have interesting distributions. There are only two genera that occur both in Africa and America: *Elaei*s and *Raphia.* The genus *Raphia* has about 27 species in Africa and one, *R. taedigera,* in tropical America. *Raphia* species are mostly found in swamplands, but one, *R. regalis,* occurs in hill slopes in the tropical rainforest of Africa. This species has leaves reaching 25m – considered to be the longest in the plant kingdom. Raffia fibre is obtained by stripping off the cuticle and hypodermis (the outer parts) from the emerging leaflets. It is much used in Africa for baskets, hats, mats and cord, and is exported for garden twine and weaving. Palm wine is obtained by tapping the inflorescences of various species of *Raphia.* It is interesting to note that both the bicontinental genera *Elaeis* and *Raphia* have a disjunct distribution in Central America and northwestern Colombia, on one side of the American continent, and in the lower Amazon on the east of the other side. This unusual distribution of these two genera is surprisingly similar.

Rattan Palm, Benin, Africa.

Lianas

Lianas – woody vines – abound in tropical rainforest. There is an area of Amazonia between the Tapajóz and Xingu rivers where the vegetation is termed 'liana forest' because of the abundance of vines climbing over the trees. The reason for the dominance of lianas in this region is uncertain, but it is thought to be connected with past disturbances.

Lianas are more common in the forests of Amazonia than in Malesia, but they can be found in all major rainforest areas. Often the trees are bound together by the massive ropes of lianas that spread from one tree to another; if a tree is blown down or felled, it often brings many others down with it because they are all roped together by the lianas. There are certain plant families where lianas abound, such as the trumpet creeper family Bignoniaceae and the Malpighiaceae. Lianas need to be flexible in order to climb and to be bent about when the host trees are blown in the wind. Different lianas have different strategies for growing and reaching up the forest canopy. Some start as small treelets with erect stems and then, when they reach a certain height, turn into vines. Others put out tendrils soon after germination and grasp onto any available support, while others germinate in the tree crowns and put down roots towards the ground.

Liana with trailing epiphytes.

Lianas seem to have an interesting chemistry and the useful substances discovered in them have been put to use by the South American tribes. Many of their medicines, fish poisons, arrow poisons and hallucinogens come from species of vine. Perhaps one of the best known is the arrow poison, curare, that was adapted into Western medicine as a muscle relaxant for surgery. Curare is a complex mixture made principally from the bark of lianas from two different plant families: the moonseed family, Menispermaceae and the strychnine family, Loganiaceae.

Perhaps the best-known and most beautiful tropical vine is the jade

Lianas, Upper Amazon, Bolivia.

or emerald vine (*Strongylodon macrobotrys*) from the rainforests of the Philippines. This vine is a member of the Leguminosae (bean) family. It has hanging inflorescences up to 90cm long, full of greenish jade coloured and almost luminescent flowers. The unusual, almost unique, flower colour is linked to the fact that it is bat pollinated. The stunningly beautiful jade vine is now much cultivated in botanic gardens around the world and attracts many visitors when it flowers. In its native habitat, the jade vine has become very rare because of the extent of deforestation in the Philippines.

Slipper Orchid, Borneo.

Epiphytes

Another difference that contributes to the appearance of rainforest is the presence or absence of epiphytes. In the American and Asian rainforests there are many epiphytes, but in Africa they are much less abundant. One reason for the abundance in the American forests is the explosive radiation of the bromeliads (pineapple family). There are over 2,000 species of bromeliads in the Americas and they tend to occur in great abundance along the branches of the trees, especially in wetter areas. Apart from a single recently dispersed species, the Bromeliaceae does not occur in Africa and Asia. Perhaps the historically drier climate of Africa contributed to the reduced number of epiphytes. In the Americas there are several other groups of plants that contribute abundantly to the epiphyte flora, especially orchids, aroids and ferns.

In Malesia there are not nearly so many epiphytes distributed along the branches of the trees, but there is an abundance in the crotches of the branches where the characteristic birds–nest ferns occur (*Asplenium nidus*). This different positioning of the epiphytes is one of the most striking visual contrasts between the forests of South America and Asia.

Although there are comparatively fewer epiphytes in Africa, there is still a considerable number. A study in Liberia found 153 epiphytic species growing in 47 species of tree; 66 percent of these were orchids, 25 percent were ferns, and the remaining 9 percent were a mixture of other epiphytic plant families.

Although they are called air plants, epiphytes do not live on air and water alone. Much organic matter accumulates around the branches and forks of the trees where they grow and this decomposes to form pockets of soil. In addition, ants and termites often carry small particles of soil up into the trees. Since these humus-rich epiphyte gardens form on some of the large tree branches some trees also make use of this source of ready nutrients and put out roots from their branches to absorb the goodness.

Orchid, Borneo.

Bromeliad, Lower Amazon, Brazil.

STRANGLERS are another form of epiphyte, usually beginning from the sprouting of a seed deposited on a tree branch in the droppings of a bird or a mammal. As the young seedling grows as an epiphyte it sends a series of long roots down towards the ground. Once these roots reach the soil the plant is no longer strictly an epiphyte and it begins to absorb nutrients from the soil. The roots then thicken and gradually put out a network of tendrils that entwine themselves around the host tree, gradually smothering its host. The most common stranglers are various species of fig. In Africa, figs are the only stranglers, but in South America a few other plants have also evolved this strategy. Other common stranglers are *Coussapoa*, another member of the fig family and various species of *Clusia* in the St-Johns-wort family.

BROMELIADS are fascinating plants. They can either be terrestrial or epiphytic and there are many species exhibiting both of these habits in South America. The string-like Spanish moss (*Tillandsia usneoides*) is a bromeliad, but most have thick leaves arranged in a tight cluster. This acts as a tank which traps rainwater. In the dry season this is one of the few places where water is available in the forest, so it is not surprising that a large number of organisms have adapted to life in bromeliad leaf tanks. There are many small micro-organisms, and even species of the insectivorous bladderworts (*Utricularia*), that are endemic to these forest reservoirs. Some species of poison arrow frogs (*Dendrobates* and *Phylobates*) deposit their tadpoles in bromeliad water tanks.

One genus of Bromeliaceae, *Brocchinia*, in the highlands of Venezuela has become carnivorous and digests insects that end up in the water in a similar way to *Nepenthes* from the Asian rainforests. Many bromeliads have rather showy flowers, often with red bracts, to attract their humming bird pollinators. This has led to many bromeliads being cultivated in tropical gardens or as house plants.

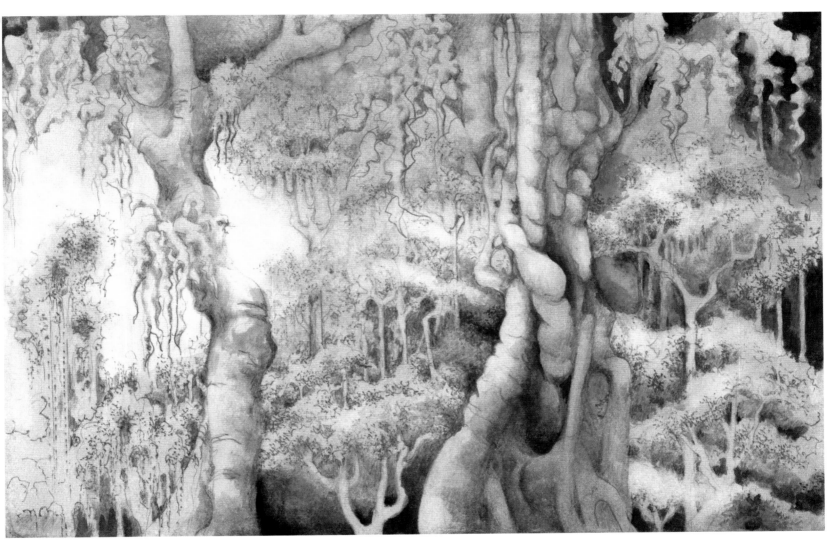

Strangler fig, Borneo.

Pollination

There is an interesting difference in the abundance and distribution of pollinators between the Asian and American rainforests. This must be partly due to the predominance of one plant family, the dipterocarps, in Malesia. Most of the dipterocarp flowers are pollinated by the tiny insects called thrips. These weak, flying insects visit the flowers and become dusted with pollen. They can only fly short distances to other trees, but the distribution of the pollen is aided by the fact that the flowers shed their corollas, which are carried by the wind, often with a load of thrips on board. Once these plant parts settle on the ground some distance from the source tree with the thrips dispersed further afield than they could travel on their own, they fly up into another tree carrying their cargo of pollen to the flowers.

In South America there is a great variety of different pollinators that, in general, are much larger animals than thrips, including bats, humming birds, beetles, large bees, butterflies or hawk moths. It is by no means just small insects that pollinate the plants of the Asian forests.

BATS pollinate some species of trees in all three major rainforest areas. The infamous pungent durian fruit develops because its flower is pollinated by the bat *Eonycteris spelaea.* This same species of Malesian bat also pollinates many other species, such as the common mangrove forest species of *Sonneratia* and the petai *(Parkia speciosa). Parkia* is a typically bat-pollinated genus of the bean family with species in Asia, Africa and America. It must have had a long period of co-evolution with bats. Since bats navigate by sonar rather than sight the flowers of bat-pollinated trees need to be readily accessible. In the case of *Parkia speciosa* they are borne on inflorescences that stick up above the branches of the tree crown. The South American *Parkia pendula,* the visgueiro tree, has inflorescences that hang down on long stalks below its very flat crown. The red pompom-like flower clusters are

Bees pollinating pendulous inflorescences.

Fruit bat.

thereby easily available to the bats, which become dusted with pollen as they drink the nectar from the flowers. The flowers are readily accessible to the bats whether they rise above the crown of the tree or hang below it; species of *Parkia* have developed both strategies.

In Africa the species *Parkia biglobosa* and *P. bicolor* are both pollinated by at least six species of bats. *Parkia biglobosa* has inflorescences that project out laterally from the crown. The flowers, which are produced while the tree is leafless, hang down from the inflorescence branches. Botanist Helen Fortune Hopkins, who climbed many *Parkia* trees to study their pollination, found that the bats visiting the African species came to the flowers in an upright position whereas those visiting *Parkia pendula* in the Amazon were up-side-down on the flowers.

The habit of bearing the flowers on long pendulous inflorescences is termed flagelliflory and it occurs in a number of unrelated species in the rainforests of the Americas. The cutia nut (*castanha de cutia*, *Couepia longipendula*) is another example of flagelliflory. This species belongs to a genus of the family Chrysobalanaceae with 75 species that are mostly pollinated by hawk moths, but two Amazonian species of the genus have developed flagelliflory and are pollinated by bats. The cutia nut has a large oval fruit and the kernel is oil rich and is used locally for cooking and lighting. A close relative of *Couepia* is the genus *Maranthes* from the rainforests of Africa. This genus does not exhibit flagelliflory, but a study in Ghana showed that the flowers of *M. polyandra* are pollinated by bats. In the white sand forest of Guyana the wallaba tree (*Eperua falcata*) is a dominant tree that lends its name to this type of forest. It is another member of the legume family and also has long pendulous, bat-pollinated flowers whose inflorescence stalks can be over a metre in length. Flowers that are pollinated in this way are termed chipterophilous, which means 'bat loving'.

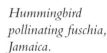

Hummingbird pollinating fuschia, Jamaica.

The 'lobster claw plant', Heliconia.

*Hummingbird pollinating
an orchid, Pantanal, Brazil.*

BIRDS are also important pollinators in the various rainforest areas. In the forests of South America many species of hummingbird, with rapidly vibrating wings, flit from one brightly coloured flower to another. Hummingbird-pollinated flowers are usually red with a tube into which the bird inserts its beak to drink the nectar from the base of the flower. Many members of the bromeliads are pollinated by hummingbirds. A typically bird-pollinated genus is *Heliconia,* the lobster claw plant, which has many species with showy, waxy, red flowers, making it popular in tropical gardens. Other bird pollinators in South America are the orioles and the bananaquits. In contrast, bird pollination is not so frequent in the forests of Malesia. In Africa however, the main flower visitors are the sunbirds (Nectariniidae). Their characteristic shimmering, metallic plumage makes them

popular with bird watchers, but they are more important for their function as pollinators of many African plants. The birds-of-Paradise (*Strelitzia*) that are related to the American Heliconias are pollinated by sunbirds. Many members of the Protea family are also pollinated by these birds. In Australia lorikeets, sunbirds, flowerpeckers and silvereyes all compete to gather the nectar from flowers and in return carry the pollen from plant to plant. The honeyeaters of Australia, New Guinea and various Pacific islands are also flower visitors as their name implies. While hummingbirds hover to drink the nectar from flowers, the Old World flower visitors mostly use a landing platform on the flower or perch on a nearby twig. An exception is the long-billed spiderhunter (*Arachnothera robusta*) of the forests of Malaysia, Sumatra and Borneo, which – in addition to its diet of spiders – also hovers to drink the nectar from flowers. It is one of the few bird pollinators of the Malaysian rainforests. Hovering is a good strategy both for taking spiders from their webs without getting entangled and for obtaining nectar.

Hibiscus, which is pollinated by hummingbirds, Jamaica.

Bouganvillea, Kenya.

DIFFERENT FAUNA ACROSS THE REGIONS

Ants

One of the features that I associate with the white sand areas of Amazonia is an abundance of ant gardens. There are some ant species that make their nests in the branches of small trees and shrubs. These nests have a variety of different plants growing in them the seeds of which resemble ant eggs and are carried from nest to nest by the ants. Typical plants of these ant gardens are species of *Peperomia* in the black pepper family (Piperaceae) and of *Codonanthe* in the African violet family (Gesneriaceae). The seeds of the plants that are carried there by the ants start to grow in small accumulations of litter or earth on the tree branches in fissures in the bark. Ants discover a young seedling and start to build their nests amongst the roots of the seedling. This gives a gradually increasing amount of humus to the plant, and as the ants nest grows so does the plant in a mutual symbiosis. When the plant sets seed, the seeds will fall into the ants' nest and so increase the number of plants. The ants have also been seen to carry around the seeds which may further increase the diversity of the ant garden. The plants flourish in this strange habitat since they live off the humus brought by the ants. These ant gardens are common throughout the lowland Amazon region. They occur most frequently in rather open areas such as secondary forests or fields and hence they also like the more open white sand vegetation.

Queen ant, Lower Amazon, Brazil.

In addition to species of *Codonanthe* and *Peperomia* other plants which grow in ant gardens are: various members of the Araceae such as *Anthurium scolopendrinum* and the aptly named *Philodendron myrmecophilum*; the epiphytic cactus *Epiphyllum phyllanthus*; various species of the Bromeliaceae or pineapple family and the attractive red-flowered members of the Nightshade family *Markea formicarum* and *M. camponoti*. The latter species is named after the commonest genus of ants that cultivate ant gardens, *Camponotus*. The most frequent species in ant gardens is *Camponotus femoratus*. There are also several other genera and species of ants that cultivate ant gardens and in some cases more that one species of ant are found in the same garden living in what is termed parabiosis. To the plant collector such as myself the ant gardens present collecting problems since these ants are aggressive and have an unpleasant sting as they protect their homes and gardens. As one touches a branch of a *Codonanthe* plant angry ants emerge from the nest in a swarm. This must certainly provide extra protection for the plants as well.

In Borneo there are also many ant inhabited plants. The genus *Dischidia* in the milkweed family occurs in the Asiatic and Pacific tropics. This is a genus of about eighty species of epiphytes and about half the species have leaves that are adapted to house ants. One group of *Dischidia* species has leaves with their edges pressed tightly against the bark of a host tree to form a tent. A second group has some of the leaves modified into cylindrical, flask-shaped structures, and yet a third group of species has flask-like leaves with a second small chamber within the outer one. The cavities of all these types of leaves are inhabited by scavenging ants in the genus *Iridomyrmex*. These ants bring debris into the cavities and it had been shown that the greater the quantity of leaves the greater the quantity of roots produced by the plants, since the roots absorb nutrients from the debris and fecal material of the ants. The nutrients from the ant detritus are important for these air plants perched high up in the trees where there is no soil. The ants construct sheltered carton (papier-mâché-like) pathways over the external roots and along the stems of *Dischidia*. In return for the nutrients, the cavities in the leaves of the plant provide an excellent home for the ants. The ants also feed on oil bodies that are produced on the seeds of *Dischidia* and through this activity they disperse the seeds in a closely evolved mutalism.

Two other Malesian genera of plants that provide homes for ants belong to the coffee family, the Rubiaceae. The epiphytic genera *Myrmecodia* and *Hydnophytum* both have a close relationship with ants. In these genera the plants have a tuber-like lower stem with a labyrinth of interconnecting chambers that are colonised by ants. The ants get a good protected home and the plants get both protection and nutrients through this mutualistic relationship. The nutrient rich material brought into the chambers by ants decays because this is facilitated by fungi that also occupy these cavities. This helps to make the nutrients available to the host plants and enables them to prosper in nutrient poor habitats. Both of these genera are common in the nutrient poor heath forests of Borneo. *Myrmecodia* has 26 species distributed from the Malay Peninsula to Fiji and all species are ant inhabited. There are over 50 species of *Hydnophytum* distributed form Malaysia to New Guinea but only some of these are colonised by ants. Plants that grow in nutrient poor habitats have evolved many different ways in which to obtain nutrients and two of the most common are carnivory and ant mutualisms.

Ants on a rambutan plant.

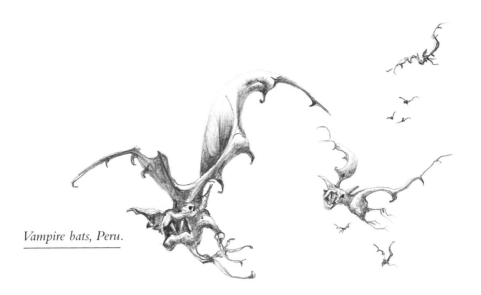

Vampire bats, Peru.

Bats

A significant difference between the forests of the Americas and those of the Old World is in the types of bats. There are two main evolutionary lines of bats, the Microchiroptera (small-hand wing) and the Megachiroptera (large-hand wing). The latter are also known as fruit bats or flying foxes. The Microchiroptera occur worldwide and are mainly insectivorous or blood eating (the vampires), though there are many variations, with different members of this group eating fish, frogs and even other bats. The Megachiroptera are confined to Africa and Asia and are mainly fruit and nectar eaters. Both groups of bats have species that are important for their role as pollinators of flowers and dispersers of seeds.

The vampire bat (*Desmodus rotundus*) feeds entirely on the blood of other animals. The bat scrapes the skin of its prey with specialised teeth and because its saliva contains an anticoagulant, the blood flows freely and its victim is unaware of the presence of the bat. Vampire bats are often a serious pest of cattle in the American tropics and they do occasionally attack people. On one of my expeditions one night I saw a vampire bat on the bare leg of one of my field assistants. At that time we were sleeping without mosquito nets because there were no biting insects along this black-water river. At first the other expedition members were rather cross that I had woken them up in the middle of the night, but when they saw José's profusely bleeding leg they were very quick to put their protective mosquito nets over their hammocks!

Frogs

Poison Arrow frogs (Dendrodobates and Phylobates) are spectacularly coloured as a warning to would-be predators that their skin is highly toxic. Indeed, the secretion from the skin of these frogs is used as an arrow poison by some indigenous tribes in Colombia. Dendrodobatid frogs normally live on the forest floor, but when it is time to breed they venture into the canopy. The tadpoles hatch on the forest floor, usually in small burrows. They then climb onto the backs of their mother who ascends to the canopy to find a bromeliad with a suitable water tank in which to deposit them. To ensure survival of some of the tadpoles from predators and enough nutrients for each of her offspring, the mother frog carefully drops a single tadpole into each water tank. She will not shed a tadpole if another frog has got there first and left a rival tadpole in the tank. If a tadpole is already present in a particular tank and it senses another frog arriving to deposit a competitor it immediately begins a warning ritual by clinging to the side of the water tank and vibrating its tail. This is enough to warn the would-be depositor and so she finds another unused water tank for her tadpole thereby giving it a better chance of survival. But the story does not end there. A week later, as the tadpoles begin to develop, the mother frog climbs back to the same plants and deposits a non-fertile egg into each tank to provide food for her tadpoles. Some species make the laborious journey to the canopy several times to ensure the survival of their progeny.

Tree frog, Borneo.

Hornbill,
South-East Asia.

Rainforest Sounds

One of the ways that I know in which of the rainforests of the world I am is by the sounds. Sound travels well and echoes through the forest.

IN AMAZONIA the two most characteristic sounds are those of the howler monkeys and the screaming piha (*Lipaugus vociferans*). The latter is a small inconspicuous brown bird that is hard to see, but has a remarkably loud call that resembles a wolf whistle. Many a female tourist has looked round to see who has been so rude as to whistle at them. The call begins with two low and well spaced gurgling notes followed by a high-pitched and startlingly loud screaming whistle that carries far through the forest. It is an extraordinary forest sound. The piha is one of the most common birds in forests near to rivers.

The second Amazonian sound resembles a jet plane taking off. The howler monkeys (*Alouatta fusca*) demonstrate their territories by their incredible roaring calls, which resonate through the forest each early morning. One can usually hear several groups all making sure that their presence is known to the others. The male howlers have a large sound box in their throat that enables them to roar so well, since they inhabit the tops of trees their sound echoes for a very long distance over the forest.

IN NORTHEASTERN MADAGASCAR I will never forget the choirs of indris (*Indri indri*) that sang to us across the forest. These large lemurs are the musicians of the rainforest for their territorial calls are much more harmonic than the calls of the howler monkeys. The indri songs are certainly the most memorable sounds of the Madagascan rainforest. They begin with a communal roar that lasts for several seconds. This is followed by the song proper, beginning with a high note followed by one or several notes of progressively lower pitch. Frequently two or more indri co-ordinate the timing of their descending phases to achieve a stable duet pattern. To hear indris singing is an experience that you

Hornbill, South-East Asia.

Toucan, South America.

will never forget. Indris are the largest of the living lemurs. They have black and white pelage and, unlike other lemurs, a very short tail. They differ from howlers in that the whole group takes part in the calls.

IN TROPICAL ASIA the rainforest the sound that I remember best is the sound of a flight of hornbills, which resembled an approaching train. This is caused because these birds lack underwing coverts, the small feathers that normally cover part of the base of the flight feathers. Another haunting sound is that of a pair of hornbills flying over the forest. I well remember standing on the summit of Bukit Belalong in Brunei looking down on the magnificent unspoiled rainforest below when a pair of hornbills flew over the treetops. The series of *ger-ok* notes from both birds echoed across the forest. When these birds settle in the trees a series of *gok* notes is made by both members of the pair, which then leads into a load roaring or barking sound.

These various sounds are part of the enjoyment of the rainforest. Unfortunately, today one all too often hears the unwelcome sounds of bulldozers, chainsaws and axes echoing across the forest as it is being destroyed to create fields or to extract the timber.

Overleaf:
Gold and blue Macaws, Peru.

Rainforest Aromas

Another feature that I associate with rainforests is the variety of different smells. The sense of smell is perhaps the sense that most evokes memories of a place.

IN THE AMAZON we often make a small slash in the tree trunk to smell the bark as a means of identification. One of my Brazilian field assistants had the nickname *cheira-pau* – tree sniffer – because this was the first thing he did each time he wanted to identify a tree. A beautifully perfumed tree is the Brazilian rosewood (*Aniba rosaeodora*), a member of the laurel family. The wood and leaves of this tree are full of the essential oil linalool, which is often used in perfumes and cosmetics. This gives the wood and bark a pleasing sassafras–like smell. Unfortunately, the rose wood has become rather rare in the forest because so many of the trees have been cut down to extract the oil for use in the perfume industry. On the other hand if you smelled the bark of another member of the laurel family, *Lauro bosta* (*Licaria* sp), you would turn up your nose with repulsion. Appropriately, the local name translates as 'Shit laurel'. Two contrasting odours from the same plant family.

IN THE MALESIAN RAINFORESTS, one of the most pleasing scents is that of the flowers of the ylang ylang tree (*Canaga odorata*). This is a fast growing tree in the Anona family that occurs in the forests of the Philippines and Indonesia and is much cultivated elsewhere for its perfumed flowers. The name ylang ylang is from the Tagalog dialect. The essential oil is steam distilled from the flowers and enters many commercial products including Chanel No 5 perfume. Thirty percent of the national income of the Comores Islands is derived from the export of ylang ylang oil. The perfume is exquisite with a jasmine/neroli/custard smell. It is much used in aromatherapy and in Samoa ylang ylang flowers are the favourite for use in leis or necklaces. In Indonesia the flowers are spread on the bed of a newly married couple. The fruit of the ylang ylang is a favourite food of various species of doves and pigeons.

Fuschia, Jamaica – this plant's sweet aroma attracts hummingbirds.

Hanging orchid, Mauritius — this plant smells mildly of rotting flesh.

In marked contrast to the pleasing ylang ylang is the durian fruit of tropical Asia (*Durio zibethinus*). This malodorous fruit smells like drains, yet it is one of the most sought after fruits of the region for it tastes of caramel, banana and vanilla (with a slight onion tang). I well remember a journey in Java, Indonesia, when after a long day in the forest we were travelling back to our accommodation tired, thirsty and hungry. Our Indonesian companions were delighted to see a roadside fruit stand with a choice collection of durians for sale. We stopped and ten of these large spiny fruits were bought and put in the back of our transit van. It was all my wife and I could do not to vomit as the powerful foetid aroma wafted through the van for the next two hours of our journey home! There are many species of durian in Borneo and each has a different taste and a stronger or weaker smell. Local people enjoy these wild species, but only *D. zibethinus* is grown commercially. The smell of durian is so strong that it is prohibited to take one on board an aircraft or into public buildings.

In Madagascar I remember the most agreeable odour of the flowers of the *Stephanotis* vine. The large, white, long-tubed flowers emit a powerful but pleasing aroma. The smells of plants have two main purposes, to attract or to repel. Both sweet scented and foul smelling flowers are perfumed to attract pollinators. Fruits such as the durian smell bad to attract bats to disperse their seeds, whereas other fruits are sweet and agreeable to us in order to attract other animals and birds to disperse their seeds. Some of the scents particularly in plant parts other than flowers and fruit are to repel predators. Many of the pleasant smelling essential oils in leaves and wood function as repellents to insect predators.

The smells of certain South American orchids function well to attract their Euglossine bee pollinators, but these insects make further use of the perfume. The male euglossines, or orchid bees, scrape off the odour from the orchid flowers and store it in special pockets in their hind legs. The somewhat intoxicated male bees then use the perfume to attract female bees for mating.

Rafflesia, *Borneo – known as the 'corpse flower', this plant smells heavily of rotting flesh.*

In contrast to the sweet smell of orchids, in the forests of southeast Asia there are two different and unrelated genera of plants, *Rafflesia* and *Amorphophallus,* that are often known by local names that translate as 'corpse flower'. This is because they do indeed smell of rotting meat. Their other claim to fame is that species of both genera vie to be called the world's largest flower. Rafflesia was discovered in 1818 on an expedition lead by Sir Thomas Stamford Raffles, hence its name. The original species, *Rafflesia arnoldii,* has the largest flower of all fourteen or more species of the genus and it can be up to 100cm in diameter and weigh 10 kilos. *Rafflesia*, an endoparasite, lives inside a host liana of the genus *Tetrastigma* in the vine family (Vitaceae). The only part to be seen is the flower, as *Rafflesia* has no roots, leaves or stem. Apart from the flower, it is just a mass of tissue inside the host plant. A cabbage-like structure begins to emerge from the stem of the vine at or near ground level. This opens up into the magnificent looking, but evil smelling flower, which has five petals and looks rather like red meat. Botanists have for a long time wondered and speculated about the relationship of this curious plant to other plant families. Recently, molecular data, using the analysis of DNA, has shown that its closest relative is in Euphorbiaceae or the spurge family and so at last the mystery of where to place *Rafflesia* in the plant kingdom has been solved.

Amorphophallus is a genus of some 170 species in the Araceae or Arum lily family that grows in the Old World tropics from West Africa through Asia to the Pacific Islands. Many of the species are rainforest plants (the name is from the Greek words *amorphos* and *phallos,* meaning misshapen penis) and the largest species of this genus is the titan arum (*Amorphophallus titanum*) from Sumatra. It has a large underground corm that puts out a huge tree-like leaf each year. Occasionally, when the plant has built up enough energy, it puts out an inflorescence instead of a leaf. The inflorescence bud rapidly shoots upward as long thick phallic-like tube. Once it has reached its full height of about three metres the inflorescence unfolds to reveal a large typical looking arum lily inflorescence with an outer sheath or spathe and an inner spadix bearing the flowers. The inside of the spathe is of a dark red meat-like colour. Once the inflorescence has opened, the foul carrion smell is emitted for about twelve hours.

The reason that both these plants have such an unpleasant smell is to attract small carrion-eating beetles and flesh-loving flies that act as pollinators. And which one is really the world's largest flower? It is *Rafflesia* because the flower of a *Rafflesia* is a single flower, whilst that of the titan arum is an inflorescence with the many small flowers inserted along the spadix. It has both male and female flowers. The female ones open first and the male ones open two days later which

Amorphophallus, *Sumatra –
the Arum lily, which smells
overwhelmingly of rotting flesh.*

avoids self-pollination. After flowering this magnificent inflorescence soon dies down and the plant goes dormant until it is ready to produce the next leaf. There are several other plants with bigger inflorescences, but the titan arum is certainly the largest in the arum lily family.

There are also many animal smells in the rainforest. Anyone who has been out in the woods or garden after a fox has passed through will be familiar with the characteristic odour they leave. I remember walking in the Sundarbans mangrove forests of Bangladesh and smelling the distinctive aroma of a tiger. Perhaps it is just as well that I only experienced the smell and not the animal that had recently passed that way. Many rainforest animals have strong scents. Most rainforest peoples have a much better olfactory sense than Westerners. I have often been amazed how the Amazon Indians pick up the trail of an animal entirely through scent. The Suya people actually classify animals by their odour. In Africa the tangy smell of a bushpig rub or the fruity pineapple smell of Peter's duiker are easily sensed.

There is a stinky bird in Amazonia called the hoatzin (*Opisthocomus hoazin*). Many of its local names refer to the unpleasant smell it emits. This primitive looking bird is about the size of a pheasant and has a distinctive crest of feathers on the back of its head. It lives in trees, mainly along the river margins, and makes a characteristic hissing sound. The hoatzin has two unusual features. The first is that the young chicks have claws on their wings that enable them to scramble back up into their nests when they fall out into the river beneath; the other oddity is that because their diet consists only of leaves, like cows, they have a ruminant system with a stomach full of bacteria to digest the cellulose; it is this that gives them their unpleasant smell. Needless to say unlike many other large birds of Amazonia, they are not eaten which helps to protect them from hunters.

Overleaf:
Pair of hoatzin, Bolivia — extremely beautiful birds, despite their unpleasant smell.

Hoatzin, Bolivia.

Leeches and Ticks

One of the big differences between the New World and Old World rainforests is in the leeches. In the Amazon there are no ground leeches. Leeches only occur in the water there. The only experience I had with them was when I was studying the pollination of the Victoria water lily and was wading in muddy lakes. In contrast, these bloodsucking animals abound in the rainforests of Madagascar and Borneo. They are waiting on the forest floor to leap onto any warm-blooded animal that passes by.

Leeches are a type of annelid worm in the order Hirudinea. They have suckers to attach to the body, and an anticoagulant that causes their host's blood to run abundantly so one soon becomes a bloody mess when covered with leeches. Anti-leech socks are definitely recommended for walking in the forests of tropical Asia!

There are many ways to remove leeches, such as with salt, alcohol or tobacco. It is important to remove them with a substance they do not like so that they let go completely and no leech parts remain in your skin.

After my first experience of these land leeches in Borneo I felt glad that most of my work is in South America where one is not bothered by these creatures. However, in the Amazon I have frequently walked into a nest of ticks. These tiny, crab-like, blood-sucking animals can be just as unpleasant as they bury into the skin. They are actually harder to remove than leeches – alcohol or tobacco is the best way to get them to release their grip. A normal routine on Amazon expeditions on return to camp is a mutual grooming session to ensure that one does not have ticks in places where you can't see them!

Banyan tree, Gujarat, India.

The Leech Pit

This is horrible.

With Bachubai I leave the boat by the river's edge and plunge into the jungle. We are following an animal track from where the animals drink from the river. This is secondary rainforest: thick undergrowth. We force our way through foliage along a thin corridor. The earth is red - and so are the leeches.

Bachubai informs me leeches in this part of the jungle are particularly vicious. He is carrying a machete and a large bag of salt around his neck, and we have wrapped ourselves up to the waist in coconut sacking.

The leech pit is the size of a dustbin lid and contains several thousand leeches. Each individual leech is about the size of your little finger. They are red, slimy and vibrate like maggots. They lie en masse on the animal track. When an unfortunate animal passes, the vibration of its movement makes the leeches jump off the ground, reaching 4-5 feet in height, to land anywhere on the passing body.

We move through the jungle slowly and with caution. I remain about six paces behind Bachubai. I happen to be looking at him when the ground at his feet explodes. There is a "crack", like the sound of a rifle bullet flying past your head. Everything turns red. I am hit, as if by a sledgehammer, and thrown backward in a blur of horror, revulsion and panic.

I try to scream hysterically but cannot find air. I am on my back jerking with shock until I feel a knee on my chest pinning me still and I am smothered in salt. The effect is instantaneous - like morphine on pain - and I start breathing again.

Bachubai had walked straight in to a leech pit. Thousands of these repulsive twisting bloodsuckers had jumped into the air behind him and hit the 'animal' following … which unfortunately happened to be me!

It felt like driving a motorbike into a swarm of bees (which I have done). You feel as if you have been shot (which I haven't). I was hit by a wall of these writhing creatures and literally blown off my feet, covered and drowning in a frenzied red ravenous entity. I lost all rational thought in instantaneous horror.

Even in such a short time enough of these have got through all my upper clothing and I am covered, and I mean covered, from my waist up in my own blood. Now I realise the reason for the coconut sacking.

Whilst recovering, I recall a story my father told me of 5 Ghurka soldiers with him in Burma, who went to sleep and never woke, as the leeches had sucked them dry overnight. At the time I had not believed him.

Now I know better.

Sunday, 19th February, 2006
Challalla, The Amazon, Bolivia

Fear

" Every man is mortal and for every man
his death is an accident, and even if he
knows of it and consents to it, it is an
untimely violence."

Simone de Beauvoire

My personal experience of fear is on two levels. The first is
survival or adrenalin based: the bullet-past-your-head,
falling-off-a-cliff, this-is-going-to-hurt fear.

And then there is the creeping fear, fear of the unknown:
the there's-something-under-the-bed, monsters-in-the-
woods, shadows-in-the-dark childhood fear. A few I
thought I had left behind…

I decide to spend a night alone in the forest. I have spent
many nights here: as a soldier, artist and traveller, but
always in a group or with a guide.   Never alone.

Orvieto, my Indian guide, is sent home, back to his village
some 20 minutes away. My hammock is slung 20 feet up a
suitable tree. Darkness descends. I gently swing and
watch the light rapidly fade. Before I realise it, I can no
longer see even my hand in front of my eyes.

Cecropia and *Musanga* trees spring up almost everywhere a gap has formed in the forest or where the trees have been felled by man. They produce a lot of shade, which enables the seedlings of other primary forest species to establish themselves underneath. Apart from *Cecropia* and *Macaranga* there are many other ant-inhabited trees in the rainforest. The genus *Triplaris,* which is common beside Amazon rivers, houses particularly aggressive fire ants. In west Africa foresters avoid trees of *Bartiera fistulosa,* the oko, which is inhabited by black ants (*Pachysima aethiops*). These ants have an extremely painful sting, the effects of which last for two days. It is not surprising that the oko is said to have magical powers to fend off black magic and turn the charm back upon the evildoer.

Secondary forest species are light demanding and intolerant of shade. They have efficient methods of seed dispersal, for example, by bats in the case of *Cecropia*. They are fast growing and often exclude other species, but since they are short lived, space gradually opens up for the more shade tolerant primary forest species. *Musanga cecropioides* grows to 11m in three years and to 24m in only nine years. Another fast-growing pioneer species of tropical America is balsa (*Ochroma lagopus*), which can reach a height of 18m in five years. It forms a soft light wood that has been much used for rafts and model airplanes. Another important pioneer species of Malesia is *Adinandra dumosa* (Theaceae), which begins to flower at the height of 2m when it is only 2 years old and continues to produce flowers continuously throughout its life. In Africa, one of the other pioneer trees is the cabbage palm, *Anthocleista nobilis*.

Toucans/Hornbills

Many people who have visited South American, African, or Asian rainforests have commented on the similarities between the large-billed toucans and the hornbills. The large Rhamphastos toucan has a yapping call that is often heard over the Amazon rainforest early in the morning. One rainforest conference I attended tried to create a realistic atmosphere by playing a recording of toucans and other rainforest creatures.

Hornbill, Borneo.

Hornbills, Danum Valley, Borneo.

When the toucan sound started, the couple in front of me commented about the unpleasant disturbance caused by 'these yapping dogs'. Toucans and hornbills are birds adapted to feed on both fruit and on small animals such as fledgling chicks and small reptiles. This has required the evolution of rather similar beaks. Hornbills use their magnificent beaks to grasp and toss insects or small reptiles into the air and then, with impressive coordination, catch them in their gullets. They also use their beaks to poke among the branches for fruit or even to keep a poisonous snake at bill's length to protect their more vulnerable body parts. Many hornbills have a spectacular protrusion on their beaks called a casque.

Both toucans and hornbills make their nests in holes in trees started by other birds or animals. The hornbills differ in habit from toucans in that they build a wall of mud to trap the female in the nest during the period of incubation. This protects the mother and the chicks from predators but must be hard work for the male as he brings home all the food for his family for many weeks.

Blow Gun Dart Poison

I came across an amazing parallel between the rainforests of the Amazon and New Guinea when I was doing an ethnobotanical study of the Maku Indians in the northwest of Amazonian Brazil. We collected samples of the poison they use for the tips of their blow pipe darts. They collect the brownish milky sap of a tree in the Moraceae or fig family (*Naucleopsis mello-barretoi*) and simply dip the darts into this sap to make them toxic. I sent a sample of this liquid to a chemist in London, Dr. Norman Bissett at the Chelsea College of Pharmacy. A few weeks later he telephoned me in New York and I could tell that he was excited. He explained that the chemical in the poison was a little-known cardiac-glycoside and that the only other place it had been found was in another genus and species of Moraceae from New Guinea, where it was also used as a blow gun dart poison. The indigenous inhabitants of the rainforest are great discoverers of the uses of plants in the forest, but it is amazing that this rare chemical has

Cloud forest, Sri Lanka.

been found and put to exactly the same use in the forests of the Amazon and New Guinea. A cardiac glycoside is a substance that affects the rhythm of the heart and so can be an effective poison. Another example of this type of chemical is digoxin, the cardiac glycoside found in the foxglove (*Digitalis purpurea*), which can be used in small doses as a medicine to correct erratic heart rhythms.

Rainforest, Sri Lanka.

Sloths and Slow Lorises

I have been familiar with sloths since my first trip to the rainforests of South America, but more recently was surprised to see a slow loris, an animal with remarkably similar habits in the rainforest of Borneo. These unrelated animals are both very slow moving, have thick fur, stubby tails and live in the tops of trees in the forest.

The sloths belong to the orders Bradypodidae (three-toed) and Magalonychidae (two-toed) and occur in Central and South American rainforests. Their diet consists mainly of leaves, tender shoots and buds from the trees in which they live, although they occasionally also eat insects and small lizards. A diet of leaves is hard to digest and so they have stomachs with multiple compartments filled with bacteria that aid the breakdown of the cellulose in leaves. Sloths are 50-60cm long, have tiny ears, big eyes, stubby tails 6-7cm long and long curved claws that help them to hang upside down on tree branches. Their hair grows in the opposite direction to most mammals, which protects them from the rain when they are upside down. Another unusual feature connected with their slow metabolism is that they descend from the trees about once every 10 days to defecate. Sloths are an ecosystem in themselves having both algae and moths living in their fur.

Slow lorises on the other hand are closer relatives to us since they are primates of the Strepsirrhine group. They are found in the forests of southeast Asia, Borneo and the Philippines. They are smaller than sloths, 21-38cm long, but have the same slow moving gait. Lorises have large eyes, small ears and a stump for a tail. They have well-developed thumbs to grip branches. The lorises are carnivores and eat insects, birds' eggs and small vertebrates; they also occasionally eat fruit. A major difference from sloths is their defence against predators. They produce a toxin which they mix with saliva; mothers will lick their young, and thereby cover them with this toxin, as a protection against predators before leaving them to go foraging for food in the forest.

Both slow lorises and sloths have slow, deliberate movements and a powerful grip, which makes them hard to remove from branches.

Sloth, Brazil.

The Great Apes and Other Primates

Some of our closest relatives, the great apes, live in the tropical rainforests of Africa and Asia. Each major rainforest region has its own characteristic species of primates. The great apes are the chimpanzees and the gorillas of Africa and the orangutans of Sumatra and Borneo. In Madagascar the lemurs are the only primates, and in South America there are no apes or lemurs only monkeys with prehensile tails. The great apes belong to the family Hominidae and are mainly rainforest beasts. All of them have been known to use tools and are extremely intelligent. They differ only slightly from humans in their DNA profile. They are all omnivores, eating mainly a vegetarian diet augmented by insects and small animals. Sadly all the great apes are endangered species, threatened by hunting for bush meat and destruction of habitat.

CHIMPANZEES – there are two species of chimpanzees: the common chimp (*Pan troglodytes*), occurring in west and central Africa; and the bonobo (*Pan paniscus*), occurring in the Democratic Republic of the Congo. The Congo River forms the boundary between the two species. The habits and behaviour of the common chimp are well known thanks to the painstaking research of Jane Goodall who spent 26 years living with and studying them. They have also been much studied in captivity and are highly intelligent – recently they were found to outperform college students in tasks requiring the remembering of numbers!

Chimps forage by day and sleep alone in nests in the trees at night. The nests are made of leaves and small branches and only mothers and nursing infants share nests. Chimps use tools to obtain ants and termites and to scare away intruders. Their diet is extremely varied, including leaves and shoots, buds and blossoms, fruits and berries, grains and seeds, husks and pods, nuts, grasses, vine stems, barks and resins, lichens, galls and larvae, ants and termites, caterpillars and cocoons, birds and eggs, honey, various small animals, minerals and water.

The bonobos are truly forest creatures, whereas the common chimp also occurs in open woodland and sometimes ventures into grassland savannas. The establishment in 2007 of a 30,570km² reserve for the bonobo by the Democratic Republic of the Congo is a good step forward in the conservation of this much endangered species, which has been greatly threatened by the bush meat trade and by agricultural projects within its territory.

GORILLAS – the other African ape is the gorilla, the largest living primate. An adult male can weigh up to 225 kilos, the females are smaller. These are truly forest creatures who are ground dwelling and only rarely climb into trees. They make their nests on the ground and sleep at night. There are two species of gorilla: the lowland gorilla (*Gorilla gorilla*) and the mountain gorilla (*Gorilla beringei*). Both species are divided into two subspecies. The lowland gorilla inhabits dense forest in lowland areas and the mountain gorilla, as its name suggests, occurs in the montane forests such as the cloud forests of the Virunga volcanoes in Rwanda. The arms of gorillas are longer than their legs and they walk on their knuckles. Gorillas live in a troop of 5–30 animals led by a silverback male who makes all the decisions, such as where they move or in mediating conflicts. Lowland gorillas eat mainly fruit whereas the mountain gorillas eat herbs, stems and roots; both species occasionally eat insects and small animals. Unfortunately, both species of gorilla are endangered through poaching for bushmeat, habitat destruction, and more recently, the Ebola virus.

Silverback Gorilla,
Uganda, Africa.

Orangutan mother and child, Borneo.

ORANGUTANS – the other genus of great apes, the orangutan, occurs only on the islands of Sumatra and Borneo. Orangutan means man of the forest in Malay, and they are truly rainforest animals. These wonderful animals with their reddish coloured hair seldom walk on the ground and are the most arboreal of the great apes. They move by swinging from one branch to another (brachiating). Like chimps, at night they nest individually in trees, and only mothers and nursing young share a nest. There are two subspecies: the Sumatran orangutan (*Pongo pygmaeus abelii*) with a narrow face and paler hair, and the Bornean subspecies (*Pongo pygmaeus pygmaeus*) with a round face and darker coloured hair. They are omnivorous but eat mainly fruit, leaves, seeds, bark and shoots, though occasionally insects and small mammals. They feed mainly in the morning and often nap in the afternoon. Orangutans are known to use tools such as a leaf cup to drink water or a leaf as an umbrella to shelter from the rain. Both species are endangered by habitat loss, the Sumatran one being listed as critically endangered and the Bornean one as endangered. Logging activities, mining and, more recently, deforestation to plant oil palm is greatly reducing the amount of available habitat for these forest dependent creatures. One million hectares of forest within the habitat of orangutans in Kalimantan, Borneo, is currently earmarked for oil palm development, and of that 210,000ha is carbon-rich peat forest. In Kalimantan, 13 percent of the 800,000ha orangutan habitat is currently threatened by oil palm development which could eradicate about 20 percent of the remaining population of the Borneo species.

Orangutan, Borneo.

SOUTH AMERICA – there are no great apes in the rainforests, but there is a wonderful variety of primates varying from the tiny pygmy marmoset (*Cebuella pygmaea*) weighing only 10-14g to the large spider monkey (*Ateles paniscus*) weighing up to 13.4 kilos. I have often encountered the latter in the Amazon forest and they can be quite aggressive either throwing down sticks from above or even urinating and sending an unpleasant shower towards the intruder in their territory. It is impossible to describe all the South American monkeys here, but the one that stands out and which I recently had the luck to encounter is the uakari (*Cacajo calvus rubicundus*). This red-faced, short-tailed monkey is confined the floodplain forests of the Rio Japurá near to the Brazilian town of Tefé. The uakari is a diurnal arboreal beast that lives in groups of about thirty individuals. They feed on seeds of immature fruit especially of members of the Brazil nut family (Lecythidaceae), ripe fruits, nectar, and some insects, particularly caterpillars. They have especially well developed canine teeth that enable them to crack open the hard fruits of Lecythidaceae. This resource is important for the uakaris because it is one of the few foods available during the height of the dry season. They generally forage in the middle to upper levels of the forest, which is often flooded beneath them, but in the dry season they will descend to the forest floor to feed on seedlings and fallen fruit. At night they climb into large trees and sleep on the highest thin branches.

All of the great apes and many other species of primates are endangered and their very existence is threatened by a number of different human activities varying from deforestation to hunting for bush meat. The loss of any of these species of primates would be serious for the ecology of the forest. As shown above most of these animals eat a large variety of fruits and seeds. Many species of plants in the forest depend upon this process for the distribution of their seeds and some even for their germination. The loss of any large fruit eating mammal is likely to have a serious effect upon the many other species with which it interacts.

Forest Giants

In both the forests of Malaysia and the Amazon the tallest species of tree in the forest has the specific name *excelsa* meaning lofty or tall. In Asia it is the tualang tree, *Koompasia excelsa*, and in the Amazon it is the angelim pedra tree (or *Dinizia excelsa*), both species belong to the Leguminosae (pea) family one of the largest families of tropical trees and the source of many other useful plants.

The tualang is a true forest giant reaching up to 80m. The record height for a tualang of 84m was recorded in Sarawak. It occurs in damp regions along rivers from Thailand through the Malay Peninsula to Sumatra and Borneo and in the Philippine Island of Palawan. The trunk has huge buttresses to support this gargantuan tree. The wood is sometimes used, but when felled it often shatters. It is also full of silica grains, which makes it hard to cut. The natives usually leave this tree standing because it is much treasured as a source of honey. The horizontal branches usually have a mass of disc-shaped honeycombs of the Asian rock bee (*Apis dorsata*) hanging from them. These bees, the largest species of honey bee, are an inch in length and they like the tualang because the branches start at 35m or above and the smooth bark makes it hard for sun bears to climb up after the honey. This does not put off the local people, however, who harvest the honey and even have honey harvesting rituals that involve mixed Hindu and Islamic symbolism. They climb the tree with smoldering branches and allow the embers to fall over the nest from above. The bees chase the falling embers to the ground and then remain there until the morning light while the natives conveniently remove the honey. A single tree can yield up to a thousand pounds of honey. Another unusual feature for a rainforest tree is that the tualang is deciduous and loses all its leaves during the dry season.

The angelim pedra tree is the tallest in the Amazon rainforest reaching up to 56m in height, a mere midget compared to the tualang. Angelim provides a better timber than the tualang and is much used for heavy construction for bridges, sleepers and ships. The wood is resistant to termite attack and to fungi. Since the trees are

An oxbow lake, Challalla, Bolivia – this occurs when the river switches its course and forms a bow-shaped lake that is independent of the river.

Baobabs,
Southern Madagascar.

convolute flowers. The Madagascan species are mainly pollinated by hawk moths, another nocturnal beast.

The tree's weird appearance is enhanced by the fact that for much of the year it is leafless and the sprawling branches do indeed look like roots. African legend tells that each animal was given a particular tree to plant; the hyena was given the baobab and planted it upside down. Another legend recounts how the devil pulled out a tree and planted it upside down. While a further local belief is that anyone who dares to pick a flower of the baobab will be eaten by a lion.

Elephant herd, the Masai Mara, Kenya.

Tapirs and Elephants

TAPIRS are one of largest of all rainforest animals. There are four species of tapirs one of which is Malaysian and the other three occur in Central or South America. So how did these obviously related animals come to be so separated geographically? Tapirs are relatively ancient mammals and many fossils of tapir-like animals appear in the early Oligocene and Eocene Ages 55 million years ago. It is thought that the American and Asian tapirs diverged into separate lines about 20 to 30 million years ago. They have changed little in the past 20 million years. They dispersed from Asia to America via the northern land connection to Central America and crossed into South America about 3 million years ago when the subcontinents joined together.

The South American tapirs are Baird's (*Tapirus bairdii*), the mountain tapir (*T. pinchaque*), which has longer more wooly fur to keep it warm, and the Brazilian tapir (*T. terrestris*).

Tapirs belong to the Perissodactyl group of odd-toed, hooved mammals along with horses and rhinoceroses. They are most distinctive for their long, fleshy trunk-like proboscis, which is flexible in all directions and is used to grab foliage. Tapirs are about 2m long and weigh between 150 and 300 kilos, depending on the species. The largest is the Malaysian tapir (*Tapirus indicus*). The American tapirs are black, grey, or dark brown in colour and the Malaysian tapir differs in having a white saddle over its back. The young of all four species have striped and spotted brown coats. This is a good form of camouflage from predators. The mature tapirs with their thick skin have little to fear from predators except humans, who like to eat their meat.

Tapirs are entirely vegetarian and eat fruit, berries, leaves and aquatic plants. Their splayed hooves enable them to work in muddy places and on riverbeds. They often go under water, either to escape predation or to browse on underwater vegetation. They are mainly nocturnal and crepuscular beasts. Unfortunately tapirs have been much hunted for their meat and their hides and so all four species are listed in conservation categories of the World Conservation Union (IUCN). Baird's tapir and the mountain tapir are considered endangered and the Malaysian and Brazilian tapirs labelled as vulnerable.

The plight of tapirs is shared by most of the large charismatic animals and birds of the rainforest. Hunters concentrate on these large species for their meat, hides, ornaments and supposed medicinal value. Added to this, the available habitat for these large beasts is constantly decreasing as more rainforest is destroyed. A recent paper by zoologist Richard Corlett estimated that hunting throughout Southeast Asia is causing a mass extinction of the large animals of the region. The situation in Africa is little better where 60 percent of large forest mammals are being captured, an unsustainable level that threatens their extirpation in the Congo Basin. The good news is that at present no large

A Mahut and his elephant, India.

mammal is threatened with extinction throughout the Amazon Basin. One of the major problems associated with the loss of these large animals is that many of them, as well as many primates, are important dispersers of the seeds of the forest plants. Dispersal is becoming reduced in areas where the large animals are rare or eliminated so the plants are affected too. The lack of these animals in some cases has the opposite effect because they are predators of some plant species and it reduces seed predation pressure. This can actually increase the relative abundance of large-seeded plant species. The natural undisturbed forest is in a good equilibrium between predator and prey and when this is altered problems begin to arise. Even the populations of the humble dung beetle can be affected by the reduction in the amount of available dung.

ELEPHANTS live in the rainforests of two continents – the elephants that roam the savannahs of Africa are well-known and much observed by both scientists and tourists, but their smaller cousin lives in the forests of Central Africa. It was only as recently as 2001 that it was decided that the forest elephants are a different species from those of the savannas. Their build is more suited for life in the forest. They are smaller, and their tusks point downwards so they don't get tangled in the dense vegetation. They communicate by using a low-frequency throb that is too low for humans to detect and is transmitted through the ground like seismic waves. In this way they can communicate over long distances.

Asian elephants are much more forest beasts than their African savannah cousins, but there too an amazing recent discovery has been made. It was long thought that the pigmy elephants of Borneo were descendents of beasts that were shipped to Sabah by a former sultan. Modern genetic studies of their DNA shows that they should be regarded as a separate subspecies that diverged from the continental individuals about 300,000 years ago. At some stage of lower sea level elephants appear to have migrated to Borneo and were then cut off from the mainland as it returned to its island status. These isolated

Pygmy elephant, the forests of Borneo.

elephants adapted to their forest habitat and, over time, evolved to a more suitable size for life in the forest. The taxonomy of elephants is more complicated than we thought even 10 years ago. There is also a forest species from Africa and a forest subspecies from Borneo that differ genetically and morphologically from the Indian elephant and that are well adapted to life in the rainforest.

Wednesday, 20th October, 2004
Bhopal, India

Ganesh

It is the Festival of Ganesh - the Hindu manifestation of charity, love or giving.

Ganesh is rather like Santa Claus.

This Hindu Father Christmas is also fat, red-faced and jolly - and lives in a grotto, though he happens to have an elephant's trunk rather than a beard!

He also has the characteristics of the Child King. The similarity to the concept of Christmas or Christ's birth is extraordinary, and enforces the case of human perennial truths.

Ganesh has 12 days of celebration - as with Christmas. Each household brings presents to its neighbour in celebration of the birth or renewal of the God Ganesh.

Family of Indian elephants, Sri Lanka.

For both 'Ganesh Day' or Christmas Day the ritual is about rebirth. For Jesus it is literal. For Hinduism it is much more powerful, symbolising resurrection as well.

Ganesh is committed to the countless rivers and tributaries of India - submerged - the effigy, made of plaster, disintegrates. To 'The River of Life' he is committed and from the 'River of Life' he will be born again.

Rivers

Universally, rivers are revered as the sustenance of life and the source of fertility and often associated with the Divine Female. It is in India and Hinduism where the divinity of rivers reaches the ultimate...

Sailing boat on the Namada River, in which I spent two weeks, India.

Nandita and orphan.

Nandita

She is heavenly: petite, graceful and sublime, with coal-black hair and eyes exuding fire. Yet elegance and calm pervade. The beauty of the Indian female has captivated me since childhood. I feel like an adoring puppy as I follow her.

Her father was 'committed' to the Namada River twenty years ago - 'buried' in Western terms. I accompany her to the spot where it happened; a place she has not visited since. We walk down to the Ghats. They are inhabitated, as on the Ganges, with limbless, diseased and discarded humans who accept their lot with tranquility and the hope of a better life to come. Nandita pauses by a pathetically wasted creature, gives alms, and accepts in return a tiny posy of nasturtium and frangipani, signifying rebirth. It is done with absolute grace - my heart cries with awkwardness as do my gestures in the face of such pitiful, yet graceful, existence. She casts the flowers to the river and they glide downstream with countless others, carrying with them love, devotion and the hope of eventual reunion.

Frangipani, Namada
River, India.

130

Hindu stupa (shrine), Namada River, India.

It is at moments like this that our humane nature is laid bare and we experience that bitter sweet feeling of understanding the human condition. That awareness of the inevitable deterioration of body and mind, but also of their existence in tandem with the eternal absolute. And yet it appears second nature to Nandita. Is this an inkling of the Divine Female?

Nandita turns to leave and I perceive in her, in those coal-black fiery eyes, something that dictates the need for an honourable conclusion to this or any other life.

She smiles... we leave. And I am, hopefully, a little closer to the Divine.

Lizards

Harry Holcroft has painted some of the most fascinating of all lizards, the chameleons of Madagascar. Lizards are universal animals and occur in many different habitats, and are quite common in rainforest areas. Lizards vary in size from a tiny chameleon from Malawi that is only 1cm long to the giant monitor lizards of Indonesia. Anyone who has visited the tropics will have seen the small lizards called geckos creeping up the walls of a house towards the light to catch the insects attracted there. Geckos have fascinating toes with suction cups, which is why they are so versatile at climbing up walls.

GREEN IGUANA – one of the lizards that one encounters most often beside Amazon rivers is the common green iguana (*Iguana iguana*). The green iguana occurs from Mexico south throughout lowland tropical America. They are up to 2m long and have a crest of spines that runs from mid-neck to the base of the tail. Under their throat they have a dewlap that is used like a flag to signal territorial rights and in courtship.

These prehistoric-looking creatures are usually to be seen basking in trees beside rivers and lakes. With their green colour they are well camouflaged and often difficult to spot. If they are in danger they will drop straight down into the river and swim away rapidly. Although it is called the green iguana they are actually quite variable in colour. Mature dominant males tend to be darker in colour than others since colour depends upon rank and also changes when they are getting ready to mate. They also tend to be darker in the morning to absorb more heat from the sun and much lighter at midday to deflect the heat. In some places iguanas are being farmed for their meat.

BASILISK – one of the most fascinating lizards that I have encountered on my travels in South America is the basilisk (*Basiliscus basiliscus*). This lizard is also known as the Jesus Christ lizard because of its ability to run over water without sinking. They manage this with the aid of their long toes on the hind feet, which have skin flaps in between.

Chameleon, Madagascar – shown here green, but it can turn bright blue when under threat.

They slap their feet on the water surface and are supported on the water by air bubbles sucked in behind the foot as it strokes downward like a swimmer in water. The lizards quickly withdraw their feet before the air bubble collapses, which accounts for the speed with which they traverse water. To perform this feat, they use a great deal of energy. Basilisks, which weigh just 90 grams, must develop a mechanical power of about 29 watts per kilogram of body weight. The maximum sustained output a fit human being can manage is about 20 watts per kilogram. The basilisk has such powerful hind legs that the researchers who study them estimated that at least 21 percent of the lizard's body mass is involved in powering hind limb motion. It would be impossible for humans to emulate the basilisk because of the size and shape of our legs and the maximum speed we can run. Even with the correct foot structure to move on before each bubble of air burst, a human runner would need to stroke downward through the water at almost 30m a second, which is well beyond our capacity. Instead we have to stand by and admire the amazing capability of this small lizard.

CHAMELEONS are most commonly found in Africa and Madagascar and are best known for their ability to change colour. These primitive animals lack ears and have eyes that can either focus separately – giving them 360 degree vision – or focus together to give good stereoscopic vision. Chameleons have very long tongues with a sticky tip. What is most remarkable is the speed with which they can extend their tongue to catch an insect. A tongue movement takes 30 thousandths of a second.

Many chameleons look exotic because of their facial ornamentation that may be either a large crest on the top of the head or nasal projections. The males are often much more ornate than the females. Another feature of chameleons is their zgodactly, meaning that two united claws face forward and three backwards,   this enables them to grip tightly to branches and   crawl through the trees. They also have prehensile tails, another good adaptation to their mainly arboreal life.

Chameleons are also well known for their ability to change colour. Contrary to popular belief, this is not to blend into the background, but is a means of communication that also expresses the fitness of the animal. Chameleons have specialised cells called chromatophores that are in layers under their transparent outer skin. The cells in the upper layer are called xanthophores and erythrophores and they contain yellow and red pigments. The layer below these is composed of cells called iridophores and it contains a colourless crystalline substance termed guanine. These reflect, among others, the blue part of incident light. If the upper layer of chromatophores appears mainly yellow, the reflected light becomes green (blue plus yellow). A layer of dark melanin containing melanophores is situated even deeper under the reflective iridophores. The melanophores influence the lightness of the reflected light. All these different pigment cells can relocate their pigments rapidly and this influences the colour of the chameleon.

MONITOR LIZARDS – the largest of all lizards are some of the monitor lizards (from the Varanidae family). These occur in Africa, Asia and throughout Malesia and the Philippines. They are considered the most advanced lizards in evolutionary terms. They are carnivorous and have special sensory adaptations that help them to hunt live prey. The largest of the monitors and the largest of all living species of lizards is the Komodo dragon (*Varanus komodoensis*) of Indonesia. These formidable animals can be up to 3m in length and can weigh as much as 70 kilograms. They have forked tongues and live largely on carrion. They are found only on the islands of Komodo, Flores and a few other small isles in central Indonesia. They can run fast in brief sprints, swim well and climb trees through the use of their strong claws.

They rarely attack humans, but in June 2007 an eight year old boy was attacked by a Komodo dragon and later died from the wounds. These lizards are considered as vulnerable in the conservation categories of the World Conservation Union (IUCN) and the Komodo National Park has been established on the islands of Komodo, Rinca and Padar to protect them.

FRILLED LIZARD – the other lizard from the Australasian region that deserves mention is the weird looking frilled lizard (*Chlamydosaurus kingii*) that is to be found in the dry forests of New Guinea and northern Australia. This large arboreal lizard is about 85cm long and has a frill around its neck. This Elizabethan looking ruff, which lies over its shoulders until erected, is raised whenever it becomes alarmed in order to scare away any enemy. The frilled lizard spends most of its time on trunks and branches of trees where it is well disguised by its brown colour. It descends to the ground only to forage.

Monitor lizard, Senegal, West Africa.

The Legend of the Royal Water Lily

The story of Nandita, told by Harry Holcroft, and the sacred river where she deposited the ashes of her father reminds me of the many traditions and beliefs of the rainforest peoples that I have met. In each place there is a rich folklore of tales of myths and origins. One of the plants that I have studied scientifically is the royal water lily (*Victoria amazonica*), named scientifically for Queen Victoria. This plant has beautiful, large, white and scented flowers that open as darkness approaches on the lakes of Amazonia. It is a wonderful sight to be in a canoe at night on a lake and watch these white stars emerging from the buds among the huge plate-like leaves of Victoria. As the flowers open at darkness the temperature inside is about 11 degrees above ambient temperature and they emit a strong fruity odour. At this time large scarab beetles arrive at the flower and enter into a cavity in the centre. Usually around six beetles are in each flower, but it can be anything from one to thirty in a single flower. The beetles are contented there with the warmth and special starchy food tissue in the flower. During the night the flower closes and traps the beetles inside. During the next day the flower gradually changes colour from white to deep purplish-red. That evening at darkness they open again now a different colour, with no scent and at ambient temperature. At exactly that time pollen is released from the anthers and as the beetles emerge, sticky from the plant juices, the pollen adheres to their bodies and is carried on to the next white flower that they enter. In this way pollination of the water lily takes place through this close relationship with a species of beetle.

That is the science of Victoria, but the indigenous belief about this plant is equally interesting. There once was a chief who had a very beautiful daughter and many young men came to ask him for her hand in marriage. The chief consistently refused and ardently protected his only daughter from the advances of

Water lily, Amazon, Peru.

her many suitors and this made her sad. In the evenings it was her custom to go down to the lake and take a bath. One day she saw a beautiful reflection of the moon on the water. She fell in love with the moon and went down to the lake with much enthusiasm each evening to talk to her lover. However she noticed that he was getting smaller and then one day she returned from her bath very sad because her lover was no longer there. Everyone in the tribe noticed how sad and unhappy the chief's daughter had become and that some days she did not even go down to the river to bathe. Two weeks later she did go back to the lake and was overcome with joy when she saw her lover shining brightly in the lake. Immediately she plunged in on top of him, but as she could not swim she drowned. There was great sadness in the tribe, but the following year a beautiful series of stars appeared on the lake, the white flowers of the water lily.

Star lily, Amazon, Brazil.

Familiar Rainforest Products in Daily Life

Long before the world was brought closer together through the current phase of globalisation, many rainforest products were familiar to most people in Europe and North America. I will mention just a few from each of the major rainforest regions.

THE AMAZON – perhaps the best-known and most used Amazon product is rubber. Although there are more than 2,000 species of trees that produce a rubber-like substance, over 90 percent of the world's rubber comes from the Hevea tree in the spurge family. This tree, *Hevea brasiliensis,* is known as the Pará rubber and is abundant throughout the Amazon rainforest, especially in the seasonally flooded areas. The bark of the tree is full of a white milky latex, which is the basic material for rubber. Many tropical trees are full of this white sticky sap and it affords protection against predatory insects by gumming up their mouth parts. Once a rubber tree has grown for about eight years it is ready to start tapping. The rubber extractor has to cut into the bark at exactly the right depth to cause the latex to run, without killing the tree. Early visitors to the Caribbean and South America found that the natives used rubber to make shoes, balls, containers and to coat fabrics. Charles Macintosh used the substance to coat the raincoats that still bear his name, but the greatest discovery about rubber was made by Charles Goodyear who invented vulcanization. This process of heating rubber with sulphur stabilises it and led to many new uses, such as for tyres. Rubber was originally harvested from wild trees throughout the Amazon region. It caused both great wealth and great distress as many indigenous peoples were bondaged into virtual slavery to extract the latex. In 1872, Sir Joseph Hooker, Director of the Royal Botanic Gardens, Kew, sent Henry Alexander Wickham to Brazil to collect the seeds of rubber trees. Wickham succeeded and, with permission, brought seeds back to England. Only a few germinated, but the surviving plants were enough to establish plantations in Southeast Asia in Sri Lanka and Singapore. Rubber plantations have never thrived in the Amazon

Peepol trees, Amazon.

because of a number of endemic diseases such as a leaf rust fungus. Fortunately, the seeds did not transfer any of the native diseases and so the Asian plantations flourished, much to the benefit of Malaysia, though to the detriment of the Amazon economy, as Brazil lost her monopoly of the product.

Chocolate comes from a plant of the Central and South American rainforests named *Theobroma cacau*. The seeds of cacau were still used as currency in the Yucatán until 1850. The flowers of cacau are produced on the trunk and arching branches of these low trees. They are pollinated by small flies. The chocolate is made from the seed and it contains a complex mixture of chemicals including the stimulants theobromine, caffeine and the muscle stimulant theophylline. The preparation of chocolate from the seeds involves fermentation, drying and the separation of fats from the product.

There are many other familiar products that have come to us from the rich botanical diversity of Amazonia, for example vanilla and the medicines quinine and curare. Remember the Amazon rainforest when you eat vanilla or chocolate ice cream.

AFRICA – our other favourite stimulant, coffee, comes from the forests of Africa. The coffee plant is a shrub in the aptly named genus *Coffea* in the Rubiaceae or madder family. Commercial coffee is produced from the seeds of two species: *C. arabica,* originally from Ethiopia, and *C. canephora* from the Congo region. The fruit contains two seeds or beans surrounded by a fleshy pulp. Commercially, the beans are heated and roasted in rotating drums. The roasting affects some of the chemicals in the beans that are responsible for the aroma. Various varieties of green beans are blended   and roasted together to achieve the best flavour. The stimulatory effect of coffee is from the alkaloid caffeine.

Coffee has the reverse history of rubber since the French transported a single plant to Martinique and this was the source of the huge coffee plantations of Latin America. Brazil lost rubber, but gained coffee through the nefarious activities of the colonial powers.

Saal forest, India – used as building materials and for thatching, and the sap is medicinal, acting in a similar way to aspirin.

Coffee consumption in Europe really began in the 17th century and by 1775 there were over 3,000 coffee houses in London alone. Today, the largest producers of coffee are Brazil and Colombia, but some very tasty specialist crops are grown in such places as the Blue Mountains of Jamaica and in Kenya.

Two other important products from Africa are the cola bean, which is used in cola drinks, and the African oil palm, which is in many supermarket food products.

Pendanus Palm, Côte d'Ivoire, Africa – used in the same way as rattan cane to make matting and baskets etc.

Banana plant, Malaya.

ASIA – the forests of Asia also bring many favourite products into our daily lives. Perhaps the best known and most popular is the banana (*Musa* species). The bananas of commerce have been highly bred, first by indigenous peoples, and then commercially. The wild relatives of the banana grow in the rainforests of southeast Asia and have hard seeds embedded in the pulp. The commercial banana has been bred and hybridized so that the fruit no longer contains seeds. This means that bananas must be propagated vegetatively from the shoots that are produced at the side of the plants or by tissue culture.

Though the banana looks rather like a small tree, technically it is classed as a herb. It does not have any woody tissue and the soft stem is formed from the leaf bases. Bananas grow quickly and are often planted together with cacau to shade the young cacau plants.

Overleaf:
Saal rainforest,
Maharashtra, India.

145

Unfortunately, the result of high banana sales means that much of the Central American rainforest has been cleared to grow bananas. They are usually cultivated using a vast number of chemicals to kill pests and prevent diseases. If we bought only organically grown and sustainably produced bananas and other tropical fruits it would greatly benefit the rainforest. Several other commonly used fruits come from the Malesian rainforests. There are many wild species of mango (*Mangifera*) and of citrus that are native to this region.

Much of our cane furniture is made from rattan. Rattans are climbing palms that are common in the Malaysian rainforest and also occur in Africa. There are about 150 different species of rattans in Borneo alone. Rattans generally have very spiny stems and so to obtain the cane the trunks are first de-spined and then boiled. This yields a long regular fibrous stem that makes a light-weight cane that is strong and durable when used in furniture. Different species of rattan yield canes of different thicknesses and of variable flexibility. Rattans are a major export of Indonesia and Malaysia; these two countries exported about 125,000 tonnes of rattan and rattan products during the 1990s. Much of the rattan is collected from the wild and this is threatening some species with extinction, although some efforts are now being made to grow rattans in plantations to take pressure off the wild species. Locally, rattan cane has many uses, such as to make baskets, mats, ropes, fish traps, hats and other craftwork.

Stimulants and Halucinogens

One of the things that has intrigued me about rainforest peoples is their ingenuity in discovering a large range of narcotics and stimulants. These vary from stimulants like caffeine – which keep them going through a hard day of work or hunting – to strong hallucinogens, which are generally a part of their spiritual and religious life.

STIMULANTS – just as we like to start the day with a good cup of strong coffee, many Amazon tribal people begin their day with a stimulant. Perhaps the best known is guaraná, made from the seeds of

Lake Titicaca, Peru.

used to help group cohesiveness and survival, as well as during puberty rituals marking the transition to manhood. Pituri is a member of the Solanaceae or nightshade family and is also a source of alkaloids – including atropine, which occurs in many of the Solanaceae such as *Datura* – which are used as hallucinogens in the Andes region. It also contains the alkaloids hyoscine, hyoscamine and norhyoscyamine, the effects of which are depression, immunity to pain and altered states of consciousness. (Hyoscine was widely used as a childbirth anesthesia in North America until the 1940s.) Apparently pituri was traded over long distances throughout Australia as it was so important to aboriginal culture. Pituri had many other uses than for rituals. Kangaroos and emus were caught by strategically placing pituri water – when the animals became stupefied and walked in circles, they were easy to catch.

Upper Amazon, Bolivia

Spirituality

Harry has recounted his visit to a shaman and so must I. I have had
the privilege of visiting many shamans in my travels amongst the
indigenous peoples of the Amazon, but perhaps one stands out more
that any other. Strangely enough this was when I was in the Oriente
of Ecuador leading a small group of tourists from the Friends of the
Eden Project where I work. Because we got on so well with
Cristobal our Achuar guide, he arranged for the whole group to visit
the shaman of his village, an unusual privilege for a tour group. The
Achuar are a proud people who are striving to protect their lands
from the exploitation of petroleum. As part of their endeavour to
develop an autonomous economy, they are also
in the process of taking over the running of the Kapawi tourist lodge.

We were taken by canoe across the river, away from the tourist
camp area, and walked up the steep bank of the river to the village,
which is sensibly isolated from tourist activity. We had been prompted
by Cristobal with the correct words of greeting and were than sat

Lake Titicaca, Peru – not the source of the Amazon, but very close to its watershed.

down in a semi-circle in front of the shaman. As we watched, not to be hurried, the shaman carefully finished putting on his face paint in the correct patterns using an old broken mirror. Once this was done our guide was allowed to make a long speech of presentation about who we were. After this the shaman replied and through an interpreter we listened to his words of wisdom. He explained that because we were people of some influence in the outside world, he had called us here to ask for help. He then made a passionate plea for us to assist the Achuar in their fight to fend off the development of petroleum exploitation in Achuar territory. As the talks proceeded the shaman's wife passed around a gourd of chicha, their local fermented beverage made from corn. I did not tell the group until afterwards that the fermentation is started by having one of the young girls in the tribe chew the dough to start it off! This visit to a shaman is one that I shall never forget because of the way in which the shaman used our visit to state his case so clearly. There is no doubt that it helped to make all of us more determined to defend the rights of indigenous peoples.

The Lagoon, Cotonou, Benin, West Africa – stilt houses of the Gauvé people.

Part III

PEOPLE OF THE RAINFOREST

Lake Volta – Ghanaian women doing their laundry in large copper pots.

No description of the rainforest would be complete without something about the role of the people who live in these areas. There are about 50 million indigenous people living within the rainforests of the world. Each major area of rainforest has native people who live there and had adapted to life in the forest long before their territory was invaded by Western colonialists. These people depend on the forest for their food, shelter, medicines and many other amenities.

There are, amongst others, the so-called Indians of the Amazon, such as the Yanomami and the Kayapo; the many forest tribes of Africa, including the pygmies who have been there far longer than the Indians of South America; the natives of New Guinea such as the Huli of Papua New Guinea; and the aboriginals of Australia. What we have left today is a mere remnant of the many nations and cultures that developed in the rainforest. For example, it is calculated that in pre-Columbian times there were at least 6 million indigenous people in the Amazon region of Brazil. This was reduced to as few as 200,000 by the mid-20th century through capture of their territory, warfare, slavery and the spread of Western diseases, to which they had little or no resistance. Today, the survivors are better protected and the population is on the increase in Brazil, but the area has already witnessed the loss of many individual tribes, much culture and many languages. It is estimated that by the end of the present century, half the languages of the world will have become extinct through pressures from Western society.

A fact that stands out to me is that where there are native peoples, the rainforest remains largely intact. Some of the best forest in the Amazon region is within the reserves for indigenous people and this is certainly also true in New Guinea. Though these communities do harvest extensively from the forest and fell small areas for their agriculture, on the whole they live in harmony with the forest ecosystem and do not destroy their livelihood. The indigenous peoples are in touch with nature, whereas the people who have

Chinese Gooseberry – which is eaten in quantity in Borneo.

An iban 'langhouse' – meaning in Malay 'come together' – in Borneo.

replaced them are often disconnected from nature and are compelled by greed to harvest more products or to destroy more forest. Rainforest peoples usually lead a communal type of life in which individual possessions take no part. The colonizers, whether missionaries or businessmen, seek to change this communal lifestyle and introduce ownership, commerce and the stopping of semi-nomadic existence. Worse still is the destruction of the animist beliefs of these people that so often give rise to their environmental consciousness. As this acculturation increases and contact with the environment is lost, even people of indigenous extraction lose touch with their environment and join in with its destruction. The lifestyle of rainforest peoples is generally semi-nomadic and, as resources are depleted, they move from one location to another. This allows time for the forest and the animals to recuperate. As the territory of indigenous peoples is reduced, they no longer have the space to move around and their sustainable system breaks down. One of the best ways to conserve the rainforest is not to exclude local peoples from reserves, but involve them in the conservation from within the reserves. They have many generations of experience of living with the forest.

161

Slime...

Myoxomytes, or ambulant self-activating protoplasm - or, to you and me - slime moulds.

In the rainforest they are everywhere. Within the detritus of the forest floor they exist as single-celled individuals, like amoebas.

But when their immediate conditions grow difficult - or optimum (scientists cannot explain) - they coalesce to a central gathering place and become a slug, similar to the one you meet on your lettuce.

This piece of living entity has no brain, no central nervous system, or heart - nothing that makes it logically work. And yet, it is a working community.

Having coalesced from over a billion individual cells, it manages to direct itself to sunlight, and reconfigures itself to form a stalk, on top of which it forms a bulb like a plant, which blows at the appropriate moment, dispersing the original billion individuals to start all over again.

How may of these different things do rainforests contain?

Countless billions.

...and Slums

Slums too are everywhere and their growth and dispersion appear incredibly similar to that of the slug.

Across the world people exist as individuals, despite village or urban life. When conditions grow difficult or optimum, (economists cannot explain) individuals coalesce to a central gathering point.

As is true of every major world city, Mumbai has hundreds of slums. I will take as an example one on Calaba Bay.

Similar to New York, A World Trade Centre in the form of twin towers was constructed in 1995. At the construction site, the labourers, artisans and tradesman involved in the building of the towers, were housed in small hutments on land adjacent to the site.

Many of these workers are itinerant, moving from construction site to construction site. They originate from homes in villages in neighbouring states, hundreds or even thousands of miles from Mumbai. In order to send money back to their families in these distant villages, they are content to work and live in the most appalling conditions. Vast underground wells were sunk to provide water and lanes and pathways cleared. Finally, a tall barbed-wire fence was erected around the perimeter. The legal slum was born. Now it grows.

Drawn by the regular wages the workers can spend, as well as the plentiful supply of fresh water, squatters soon arrive and settle outside the fence line. Entrepreneurs establish tea/chai shops and small grocery stores, attaching these little shops to the fence. Workers from the legal compound stoop and crouch through the gaps in the wire to spend their money.

Next come vegetable shops, tailors, and little restaurants. Gambling dens and other dens for alcohol or "charas" follow. Each new business clings to the fence, until there is no space left on the fence line. This illegal slum begins to grow outwards into the surrounding acres. In time there are 8 to 10 squatters for every legal worker in the compound. 30,000 in all, and the division between legal and illegal slums becomes blurred.

To worker and squatter alike, the company fence is arbitrary and irrelevant. Workers, not permitted to bring immediate family into the legal slum, invite their relatives to squat near them beyond the wire. Friendships flourish among the children on both sides and marriages of love and arrangement blossom. And because fire, flood and epidemics don't recognise wire boundaries, emergencies in one part of the slum require the close co-operation of all.

The slum, like the slug, becomes a living entity, with no command, or heart or central nervous system, nothing that makes it logically work, but like the slug it does - beautifully.

And then the twin towers are completed and the slum is cleared. Bulldozers arrive. Tens of thousands of individuals are dispersed - to start the process, just like the slug, all over again at another location.

Calaba Bay, slums surrounding the World Trade Centre in Mumbai, India.

An Indian Hospital

Mumbai

Whilst on my travels, I have a serious Asthma attack.
Luckily, I am with friends in their apartment in Mumbai,
and they arrange for emergency admission to hospital.

I am 'trolleyed' to a white cell, just big enough to hold one
old iron bed, accompanied by drips and oxygen. The door
is closed and I am left, morphine and oxygen taking their
effect.

There is a knock at the door. In comes an Indian with a
blue peaked cap, white gloves, white suit and white
'booties'. He has a broom. He sweeps the floor with a
tremendous flourish, salutes, smiles and then leaves.

5 seconds later in comes another Indian with a green
peaked cap, white gloves, white suit and white 'booties'. He
has a wet mop. He mops with equal flourish, salutes, smiles
and leaves.

Another 5 seconds pass and in comes another Indian
dressed in the same garb, but with a brown peaked cap. He
holds a dry mop, and polishes with even more flourish and
vigour, then salutes, smiles and leaves.

My floor is gleaming!

A nurse enters. Tall, beautiful and with shiny
white teeth and brimming with health. So white so
starched and so crisp, she crunches her way to my
bedside and does what nurses do with pulses, pumps
and thermometers.

Minutes later more crispy, crunchy, starchy, white nurses
scrub me, wash me, polish me and I am left glowing in a
gleaming room.

Now this is good medicine!

The Yanomami

The Yanomami are one of the largest remaining tribes of Amazonia and were, until recently, isolated from other cultures. They inhabit the frontier region between Brazil and Venezuela and the population is almost equally divided between the two nations. They live in large community roundhouses called *yanos* or *shabonos*. They speak a language that is unrelated to any of the other major language groups and so their origin is unclear. Unlike other Amazon tribes, their staple crop is plantain bananas rather that cassava. Perhaps this came about because they are more recent agriculturalists who only developed this skill after bananas were introduced to South America in post-Colombian times. Although they cultivate crops, the Yanomami are truly forest-dependent people, and hunting and gathering of forest products is still very much part of their daily life. They hunt birds, monkeys and other animals with their poisoned arrows, they gather fungi, grubs, frogs and almost anything that is edible.

I had the privilege of spending considerable time amongst the Yanomami in the 1960s and '70s. At that time they still really had a stone age culture that was well adapted to life in the forest. Since then they have had much contact with invading gold miners, government officials, missionaries, anthropologists, journalists and even botanists like me. This has led to considerable changes in their traditional ways of life. The miners, in particular, brought death and many diseases to the Yanomami. For example, in 1993 many inhabitants of Haximu village were massacred by miners.

On an expedition in 1970, the young guide that took us up to the top of Pico Rondon in Yanomami territory was called Davi, the son of a shaman who was learning Portuguese from a government nurse. Since then Davi Yanomami has become an outstanding leader who has stood up bravely for the rights of his nation and other indigenous people of Brazil. He has travelled widely and received several international awards for his work, drawing attention to the atrocities of the miners and fighting for recognition of territorial rights. I met Davi twice while he was campaigning in the UK, the last time as recently as November 2007, when he was drawing attention to yet another invasion of miners into their lands. Through much international pressure and the work of Survival International, the Yanomami Park was created in 1990, giving them back their traditional lands, though it is still under constant threat.

One of my most exciting and difficult expeditions was when we walked 280km with a group of 19 Yanomami across their territory from one missionary airstrip to another. Over a period of two months we walked for half of each day and then worked on collecting plants and studying Yanomami ethnobotany for the remainder of each day. We visited many Yanomami villages, some of which had never seen a white man before. One of the aspects we studied was their use of many species of edible fungi. Most tribes in Amazonia eat few fungi, but we have now classified 34 species used by the Yanomami. Each edible species ends with the suffix −*amo*, for example samisami-

A Penan family fishing boat on the Miri River, Borneo.

amo (*Polyporus aquosus*) or uikassi-amo (*Favolus brasiliensis*). Non-edible fungi are all termed unishelidá (meaning 'no good'); indigenous taxonomy is often based principally on use.

On one expedition we were able to attend a Yanomami feast celebrating their harvest to which a nearby village had been invited. Large quantities of food and sugar cane juice were served. For their dances they decorated their bodies with paint, feathers and flowers, and the festivities last almost the whole night. The Yanomami have the reputation of being fierce due to the documentation of their fighting by anthropologist Napoleon Chagnon. Infighting is certainly a feature of Yanomami life and raiding for women used to be very common, but they can also be friendly and hospitable, as I have found on all my expeditions amongst them. This great Indian nation hangs on rather tenuously against the many external pressures of today. Unfortunately, the governments of Brazil and Venezuela do not have adequate enforcement programmes to protect the Yanomami and to prevent the incursion of outsiders into their lands.

The Baka Pygmies

It is not just elephants that have become smaller in adaptation to life in the forest, it is also people. The pygmies of central Africa are small people whose average height is under five feet (150cm). Like the South American Indians there are many different tribes of pygmies and a great variety of languages. Pygmies are descendents of Bantu and Adamawa-Ubangi who have adapted to living deep in the forest. Two of the best-known groups are the Aka and the Baka.

The Baka inhabit the rainforests of Cameroon, Gabon and northern Congo (another different group of the Democratic Republic of the Congo are also often known as Baka). The Baka language is related to that of the Adamawa-Ubangi. The Baka are nomadic hunter-gatherers who make temporary huts of bowed branches covered by large leaves. The women gather wild fruits and honey, while the men are the hunters, using poisoned arrows and spears.

The men also use special poison to gather fish. This practice is used by indigenous peoples around the world as many plants contain chemicals that interact with the gill membrane of fish and causes them to suffocate rather than be poisoned. I have observed the use of fish poisons with the Yanomami and many other Amazonian tribes, but it is just as common among the Baka and other forest peoples of Africa and Asia. The Baka remain in an area until it is hunted out and then move on to another part of the forest, allowing time for the resources to replenish. Of course, this system only works as long as there is enough forest remaining for them move around in.

Life is communal within a Baka group and decisions such as when to move on are made by group consensus. These are truly forest people who depend upon the resources of the forest for all their needs. As a result, they have a large pharmacopeia of medicinal plants. Like most indigenous peoples, the Baka's traditional way of life is under threat, principally from loss of forest due to clearance by multinational logging companies. The Baka people have also been exploited by other more progressive groups, such as the Bantu. The government of Cameroon has even tried to enforce mandatory schooling for all Baka children. The Baka have largely resisted this, but these rainforest people are under as much threat as the Yanomami.

The Penan

Borneo is another rainforest area in which many different indigenous peoples live, most are classified as Dyak. One of the best known groups is the Penan, who live in Sarawak and Brunei. There are about 10,000 Penan. Traditionally they were hunter-gatherers living in the rainforest, though today most of them are settled in small villages of the traditional Borneo longhouses. A few individuals (around 350–500) have maintained their nomadic lifestyle, hunting and gathering in the rainforest of the Tutoh and Limbang river watersheds. Even the more settled Penan still depend on the forest for some of their basic needs, including food and medicines. The nomadic remnant live in temporary camps, made of saplings and leaves, which they occupy for a week to a month, depending on the availability of resources. They are entirely reliant on the forest for their food and trade items. However, due to external pressure and shortage of forest products, the majority have settled in villages. These semi-settled people subsist on the cultivation of rice and tapioca, and on the wild sago palm (*Eugeissona utilis*).

The traditional Penan are excellent hunters and their varied diet includes wild boar, barking deer, mouse deer, snakes, monkeys, birds, frogs, monitor lizards, snails and insects, as well as forest fruits and starch for the sago palm. They hunt with blowpipes made from the billian or Borneo ironwood tree (*Eusideroxylon zwageri*). These are carved out with incredible accuracy using a bone drill. The bore may be as long as 3m and is precise to the millmetre. The darts are made from the sago palm and are tipped with an extremely toxic poison from the latex of a tree.

The Penan drew international attention through their resistance to logging operations in Sarawak because these activities were severely affecting their lifestyle. Logging caused sediment displacement and the loss of many sago palms, as well as scarcity of game and many of the other forest resources upon which they depended. Together with Dyak commumities – such as the Iban, Kelabit and Kayan – they set up blockades to try to halt the logging. There have been large scale clashes between these indigenous peoples and logging companies, police and even the Malaysian army, resulting in death and injury to many people. This conflict continues today; on 4 April 2007 a blockade set up by the Long Benali Penan community was forcefully dismantled by the Sarawak Forestry Corporation and a special police force unit.

Though there is space here to mention just three rainforest peoples, they represent the wonderful diversity of culture that exists in the rainforests of the world. These three groups, as well as many others, are forest dependant and, in one way or another, their traditional livelihoods and their very cultures are threatened by outside influences, such as gold miners and timber companies. This is true of countless other rainforest peoples. Few, apart from some as yet uncontacted peoples in western Amazonia and in the mountains of New Guinea, are unaffected by destructive and greedy Western culture that has impacted so negatively on their lives. Rainforest peoples have practised sustainable living for many generations. This has been helped by their animist beliefs, which uphold many taboos that control their use of the resources around them. The loss of these spiritual beliefs is another way in which changes in culture have turned some of these peoples into destroyers of the forest, rather than its protectors. The Yanomami, the Baka and the Penan all have firmly held religious beliefs that strengthen their ability to live in and manage the rainforest environment.

Indian Black Soils of Amazonia

People talk a lot about virgin rainforest, but the more we explore the forests the more we learn about previous occupants of what now looks like pristine forest. Many forest peoples construct their homes of wood and thatch, which soon rots and disappears once an area has been abandoned. The remains of only a few more advanced forest cultures, such as the Maya of Mexico or the builders of the Angkor temples of Cambodia, testify to the former occupants. However, many of the soil pits that I and others have made in the middle of the Amazon forest contain fragments of charcoal and, in some cases, even pottery shards. In recent years several researchers have drawn attention to large areas of a rich dark soil that occurs in many places throughout the Amazon region. This soil is known as *terra preta dos indios* or Indian black soil. It is highly fertile and is now sought after by farmers and horticulturalists. Exactly how it was made is not known, but the soil contains a lot of charcoal and organic matter, which shows that former residents of the region had learned to cope with the poor soils of the Amazon region. However, most of the areas of black earth are now, or were, covered by dense forest. The former occupants of the rainforest were not nearly as destructive as contemporary society and, given time, the forest regenerated without the loss of many species. Before the time of colonialists there were many people living in the rainforests of the world, but the forest was still there for the colonialists to see. Few species other than some of the large animals were endangered or extinct. The indigenous peoples of the forest have traditionally been the guardians rather than the destroyers of the forest. The real devastation of the forest began largely through outside influences such as the world's demand for beef, timber and soy.

River rainforest on 'Indian black soils', Amazon, Brazil.

Destruction of the rainforest, Brazil (detail, see page 189).

Part IV

DESTRUCTION
OF THE RAINFOREST

No description of the rainforest today would be complete without some further comments on the destruction that has taken place, largely over the past 60 years. It is now estimated that about 50 percent of the rainforests of the world have been destroyed. This should be a cause of alarm for three main reasons: first, rainforest is vital for the control of the world's climate and the other environmental services that hold the world ecosystem together; secondly, although rainforest covers only about 7 percent of the land surface of the world, it holds over 50 percent of the total biodiversity; and thirdly, we are reducing our options to discover new medicines, agrochemicals, and other useful plant products as we lose rainforest species through extinction.

Rainforest is being destroyed for its timber, for colonization and resettlement programmes, for mining operations, for the extraction of oil and gas, for cattle ranches, for soybean fields and, increasingly, for sugar and oil palm plantations to feed the new craze for biofuels. Biofuels are touted as part of the solution to reduce carbon emissions and, where appropriate, they can indeed help. However, to cut down the rainforest to produce biofuel cannot be a wise way forward. Brazil, on the other hand, has an impressive biofuel programme using alcohol to fuel over 40 percent of it vehicles. This is largely based on ethanol made from sugar cane, grown outside its rainforest areas or in areas where the forest was already destroyed, and it is an example of a successful biofuel project. However, a plan to cut down most of the rainforest in the heart of Borneo to grow oil palm for biofuel would be a disaster and it is to be hoped that the environmental organizations that are fighting this project will be successful.

Rainforest destruction is taking place in all major regions and in some places it is worse than in others. A lot of publicity has been given to destruction of the Amazon rainforest and it is indeed serious, but only about 20 percent of that great forest has actually been lost so far. In other words there is still time to save a lot of it if the right measures are taken. The good news is that the deforestation of the Amazon in Brazil during the period August 2005 to July 2006 was considerably less than in previous years, dropping from 26,00km^2 in 2004–05 to 18,793km^2 in 2005-06 and down to 14,039km^2 in 2006-07, an impressive reduction of 25 percent. This is an indication that the government's 'Plan of Action for the Protection and Control of Deforestation' (PPCDA) is beginning to take effect. However, as I write this in October 2007 the satellite images of Amazonia show a huge number of fires burning in what has been another exceptionally dry year. The final figures will probably show an increase again for 2007.

Destruction of the forests of Java has been almost total and Sumatra is quickly following suite. The Sumatran tigers and rhinos, the orangutans of Borneo, the gorillas of the Congo and the manatees of the Amazon river are amongst the large charismatic animals that are threatened with extinction because of human activities.

One of the most serious losses is of the rainforest of Madagascar because it harbours so many endemic species of plants and animals, many of which are threatened with extinction. Interestingly, an area of Madagascan rainforest also demonstrates one of the important solutions to stem rainforest destruction: a programme called carbon ranching allows polluters to make up for the emissions of carbon dioxide by paying countries in the developing world to preserve their forests and, therefore, to continue to store their carbon. Madagascar is using the funds it gets from various multinational corporations to protect its forest and to fund poverty reduction programmes.

It is calculated that at present about 20 percent of the total carbon emissions of the world are caused by deforestation. This is more than is produced by the entire transport sector. This means that to halt deforestation on a worldwide basis would make a significant reduction in our emissions of carbon dioxide and other greenhouse gasses. This is probably the most compelling argument for protecting the remaining rainforest. To achieve this it would be necessary for the developed world to compensate the poorer tropical countries in some way for keeping their carbon-storing forests intact.

A coalition of rainforest nations led by Papua New Guinea and Costa Rica is promoting carbon ranching as a solution to deforestation. This would make good economic sense. The average hectare of cleared forest is valued at between $300 and $500. On European markets, carbon is trading at about $20 a ton at present. Since the average area of rainforest holds about 500 tons of carbon it is an asset worth $10,000. As a recent World Bank report said "Farmers are destroying a $10,000 asset to create one worth $200." One of the defaults of the much debated Kyoto protocol to reduce carbon dioxide emissions is that, although it created a system of carbon credits, it did not include credit for avoided deforestation. If the developed world would help to pay for avoided deforestation through a system of carbon credits, it would be a strong incentive for the poorer nations to keep their forests. This would be in the interests of all countries of the world since the rainforests are so vital as a store of carbon and for their role in the control of the world's climate system. The signs are good that avoided deforestation is now on the international agenda since there was much discussion about this – and agreement that it has a place in any successor to the Kyoto protocol – at a recent international climate change meeting in Bali in December 2007.

One of the most serious areas of deforestation, in terms of carbon emissions, is the peat forests of Sumatra and Borneo. Here there is a large accumulation of peat many metres deep underneath the forest that stores a huge amount of carbon. Recent deforestation has led to the peat being set on fire as the colonisers cleared the forest and burnt it to open up new fields. Peat catches fire and is almost impossible to extinguish since it goes on smouldering underground for many years, at the same time emitting huge quantities of carbon dioxide and other greenhouse gasses. In 2007, for example, there was a lot of peat burning in Sumatra. One of the most urgent actions to reduce carbon emissions is to stop any further burning of the Indonesian peat forests. Perhaps compensation for avoided deforestation will be the mechanism that halts the destruction of the remaining peat forests of Asia.

Deforestation is not only adding to the atmospheric carbon dioxide, in some areas it is causing more direct local climate changes. For example, the deforestation of the lowland of Costa Rica is causing a change in the climate of the highland cloud forests. The Monte Verde Cloud Forest Preserve is one of the best protected forest reserves in the world. One of the best known organisms there was the attractive golden toad (*Bufo periglenes*). I had the privilege of seeing this beautiful animal when a student of mine was working in the reserve studying the nocturnal pollination of a shrub by mice. Unfortunately, the golden toad and several other species of amphibians have now ceased to exist in Monte Verde, its only known habitat. The reason is that lowland deforestation has caused this forest, which before was always dripping wet, to have short dry periods. This was enough to send the golden toad into extinction. The problem is that deforestation in one place can also have an impact on other places. This is also true in Amazonia because the majority of the rainfall is blown into the region from the Atlantic Ocean. Brazilian scientist Eneas Salati has shown that when the rain from the Atlantic first falls on eastern Amazonia, the forest pumps about 75 percent of the moisture back into the atmosphere through the process of evapotranspiration. Only around 25 percent of the rain enters the soil and eventually flows into the rivers. This means that the rain is then blown further west and is recycled several more times before coming near to the Andes. At this high mountain chain the rain pattern changes direction and is blown south towards the agricultural areas of southern Brazil and northern Argentina. Recently there have been some years of drought, which are probably caused by the increased deforestation in the eastern parts of Amazonia, which is likely to have upset this rain cycle. So, it is clear that the repercussions of deforestation on local climate are just as serious as the effect of the added carbon dioxide to the atmosphere.

Biofuels

The latest threat to the rainforest is the world's hunger for biofuels as a substitute for petroleum-based fuel. On the surface, this would appear to be a good thing because the use of biofuels should reduce carbon emissions. Biofuels that are produced from plants grown on marginal lands will prove to be beneficial; Brazil has a successful biofuel programme based on sugar cane. Obviously to cut down any rainforest – the single most important store of carbon – in order to grow crops for the production of biofuel would make absolutely no sense at all. And yet, exactly this is occurring.

The two most common biofuel crops in tropical areas are soy and oil palm. The economic and environmental pressures to produce biofuels has meant that the price of palm oil has tripled since 2005 creating a huge incentive to plant more, and this is usually in rainforest areas. In environmental terms, converting rainforest to oil palm is senseless because it releases about 60 percent of the carbon held in the forest. It would take more that 130 years' use of biofuel to compensate for the loss of carbon in the rainforest.

I have recently returned from Malaysia, the second highest producer of palm oil, where plantations of oil palm growing in former rainforest areas now dominate the scenery. The federal government of Malaysia has prohibited the felling of further rainforest to grow oil palm, but the responsibility for the control of forest lies with the state governments. The states of Malaysia are not heeding the federal advice and in some cases even reserve areas are being ruthlessly felled and turned into fields of oil palm.

The latest news is that because Malaysia is running out of space to grow more oil palm, its land development Authority (FELDA) has announced plans to establish 100,000 hectares of oil palm plantations near to Tefé in the heart of Amazonian Brazil. Unfortunately, the potential for oil palm plantations in Amazonia is vast and already much of the Pacific coastal rainforest of Ecuador has been replaced by oil palm.

So how can we, as individuals, make a difference? We need to ensure that any biofuels we use have not been produced by cutting down rainforest, but instead use biofuels made from recycled fish and chip oil, waste biomass or from wood grown on marginal lands. The European Union has issued a directive that 5.75 percent of petrol and diesel come from renewable sources by 2010 and 10 percent by 2020. This is premature – until there is an adequate supply of ecologically acceptable biofuel we should not rush into its use, and thereby actually cause more damage to the environment; so the UK government is right to resist this directive.

Palm oil is also an important food product and the pressure of production for biofuel use is one of the major factors pushing up food prices. The use of palm oil from the rainforest or alcohol fuel from cornfields of America is causing havoc with world food prices and with the environment.

The last word goes to John Beddington, the UK government's Chief Scientific Advisor, who said recently that cutting down rainforest to grow biofuel crops was "profoundly stupid".

★ ★ ★

Through our texts and art, Harry Holcroft and I show some of the light and the spirit of the rainforest. However, a darkness still hovers over this remarkable and vitally important ecosystem because, despite many local efforts and much political discussion, the destruction continues. We know that when a certain, as yet unknown, level of deforestation is reached in Amazonia the climate will change so radically that we will lose the rest of the forest. We do not know how near we are to this point of no return, but we really do not want to reach it. We hope that this book will encourage you to continue the fight to save the light and spirit of the rainforest upon which the survival of the human race may depend.

Northern Madagascar – virtually the whole of the rainforest area is now barren.

An Eco-experiment in Bolivia

Challala is a village inhabited by The Tacana Indians
part of a group called The Quechua. They live in what
now has become a nationalised park, so in order to survive
without resorting to traditional methods of hunter-gathering they
have independently started a project of sustainable Eco-Tourism.

15 Tarzan-style cabins - reproductions of their own dwellings -
have been constructed in the trees. Individual Indians have
learned English in order to work as staff and guides for those
wishing to stay in the rainforest.

Amazingly, this sustainable development has stopped a migratory
Indian tribe from practising "slash and burn", saving miles of
rainforest. And the tribe has gained too - they now have a school
and a little hospital deep in The Upper Amazon 7 days by raft.

There are hundreds of similar endeavours. But the sad reality is that
they are drops in the ocean in comparison to the scale of destruction.

In the Amazon, a stretch of rainforest a mile wide and equivalent
to the distance from London to Basinstoke is disappearing every
day due to forest clearance in order to produce beef and soya.
Worldwide, an area the size of a football pitch is disappearing
every 5 minutes. Take this to its logical conclusion, and in 30
years there will be no rainforest left at all.

A depressing legacy for our children.

Overleaf:
Destruction of the rainforest, Brazil.

Upper Amazon, Bolivia.